1987-88 Edition

San Francisco on a Shoestring

The Intelligent Traveler's and Native's
Guide to Budget Living in San Francisco.

With Expanded Intermediate, and Splurge Sections.
NEW: Oyster Bars, Big Splurge Hotels & Restaurants,
Bars With Free Hors D'Oeuvres

Louis E. Madison

Copyright 1987 by A.M. Zimmermann & Company

Published by A.M. Zimmermann & Company, 2210 Jackson Street, Suite 404, San Francisco, CA 94115, Tel. (415) 929-7577

ISBN Number 0-912125-02-0

Cover design by Maureen Martin
Laser-printing by H.S. Dakin Company
Computer design by Matthew Holtz, author of *Mastering Microsoft Word*

Printed and bound by Economy Bookcraft

Printed in the United States of America

Contents

I. Introduction

This is the Fourth Edition of *San Francisco on a Shoestring* which has become a "staple" in the bookstores in the Bay Area, in many cities of the U.S. and in several European cities. The reason is that most people want value for their money. *San Francisco on a Shoestring* helps them find value.

At the outset, it must be pointed out that almost all restaurant prices are quoted *before* tax (6.5%) and tip are added. This brings a $10 meal to about $12, assuming a 15% tip. The same is true of hotels. The tax--which is now 11%--is almost never mentioned in quoting the price of a room.

As in previous editions, a number of listings will no longer appear. Some hotels and restaurants have gone out of business, others have been found failing in quality, some have become too expensive for what they offer. Although the inflation rate is supposed to be at a 25-year low, some restaurants have raised their prices during the past 2 years by as much as 20-30%. Some hotel rates have also gone up more than necessary and have therefore been dropped from the list. A number of hotels have refurbished and new ones have. opened. San Francisco is becoming overpopulated with hotel rooms, to the benefit of the knowledgeable tourists.

I have added a new group to the restaurants: *Bars-With-Free-Hors-D'Oeuvres*. Some bars offer entire buffets and invite you to make supper out of them. But you have to be careful with the price of the drinks. Some are as high as $4.50 and you have to decide if the ambience and hors d'oeuvres are worth that much. I have chosen those in the $1-$2.50 range (a little higher for bars in large hotels).

I have also added a new category to hotels and restaurants: *Big Splurge*. The reasoning is that everyone of us, no matter how impecunious, has one occasion that calls for a celebration--a wedding anniversary, birthday, etc--which justifies a dinner in the $15-$30 range (per person), or a hotel weekend at $40-$50 per night (per person). It being understood, of course, that these have to be *good values,* in keeping with the philosophy of this book.

In this connection, I cannot point out too often that *shoestring* does not mean *cheap* but *value.* I strive for quality in all categories but, of course, if you pay $3.95 for a lunch you cannot expect the same value as if you paid $10 (although, sometimes, you'd be surprised). So, the term *value* is relative. The terms *Economical, Intermediate, Splurge,* and now, *Big Splurge,* are also relative. For some, *Economical* might not be good enough (probably, no tablecloths and cloth napkins), while *Splurge* might just be right for the more affluent. In most cases, no matter what category you choose you'll probably wind up with more value than if you had chosen on your own.

Due to extreme competition (there are more than 4,000 restaurants in San Francisco and more are opening almost daily), many restaurants have "specials", e.g., 2-entrees-for-the-price-of-one, a complimentary bottle of wine or "early dinner" in the $6.95-$7.95 range. In addition to the "corporate rate" and club-discounts, many hotels often offer specials, usually package deals, especially in the off-season. You can find some listed in the Friday and Sunday editions of *The Progress,* in the *Bay Guardian,* in the Friday edition of the *S.F. Chronicle,* and in the tourist brochures available at all large hotel reception desks, as well as at the *San Francisco Convention & Tourist Bureau* at 5th & Market Streets.

A word about the *Miscellaneous* section at the end of this book. It will tell you where to buy books, old and new, where to get a haircut at an acceptable price, how to telephone, (beware of doing it from hotels!), which credit cards to leave home with, etc. etc.

Everything in this book has been checked and double-checked. Still, errors creep in. Restaurants close or change their hours, closing days, prices. Before going to a restaurant or hotel, be sure to telephone in advance and confirm its existence and prices. At the same time, ask for directions to get there if in doubt.

Should you run into a situation that needs correction, please let me know. Your comments will help others. If you are very pleased with my recommendations, a short note will ensure inclusion of a favorite hotel or restaurant in future editions.

Have fun!
Louis E. Madison, March 1987.

II. How to Use This Guide

Whenever possible, the street number, cross street, telephone, number of rooms of hotels, hours of operation of restaurants, museums etc., and an excerpt from the menu of eating places are shown. For hotels and restaurants the city location is also given.

As pointed out above, all restaurant prices are given without tax (6.5%) or gratuity and all hotel prices, unless noted otherwise, without the 11% hotel tax.

It is advisable to acquire a MUNI Street & Transit Map (about $1.25 at most bookstores, drugstores and newspaper stands). This will help you locate the listings more easily. If you do not have a bus map and do not know how to get to a hotel, restaurant, shop etc., phone MUNI (Municipal Railway), 673-6864, tell them exactly where you are, the street and cross street, and they will tell you which bus to take. Be patient as they are very busy and usually understaffed. A better solution is to phone the hotel or restaurant and ask them for specific instructions on how to get there. They should know.

Ratings and Locations

Ratings

* simple but acceptable
** good
*** very good
**** excellent, BEST BUY

Locations

(1) Union Square area to Van Ness, including Post, Sutter, Bush
(2) Chinatown
(3) North Beach
(4) Fisherman's Wharf, Ghirardelli
(5) Union Street
(6) Marina, including Chestnut, Lombard
(7) Lower Market (South of Market)
(8) Financial District
(9) Geary Street, south to Market
(10) Upper Polk Street, Van Ness, including Opera area
(11) Pacific Heights, Laurel Heights
(12) Japantown
(13) Geary Boulevard
(14) Haight-Ashbury
(15) Upper Market, Castro area
(16) Mission and Valencia areas
(17) Potrero
(18) UC, Parnassus areas
(19) Inner Sunset, lower Irving Street
(20) Outer Sunset, upper Irving Street
(21) West Portal
(22) Inner Richmond, lower Clement
(23) Outer Richmond, upper Clement

III. Transportation

To and from San Francisco and Oakland Airports

By taxi

This is the easiest but most expensive route--unless you are 4 or more-- about $25 between the S.F. airport and downtown and around $35 from the Oakland Airport.

Airporter Bus to SF Airport.

For taped message phone 673-2432, for further information phone 673-2434 or 877-0304 at the Airport. The bus to and from the S.F. Airport and the Terminal at Taylor and Ellis Streets (behind the Hilton Hotel) is $6 one way and $11 round-trip. The buses run from 5:30am to 10pm every 15 minutes and from 10pm to 2:40am every 20-30 minutes. Running time is about 30 minutes. *Airporter* buses also run from downtown and Fisherman's Wharf hotels. Running time 30-45 minutes. Phone for exact times and locations.

SamTrans to SF Airport

This is the cheapest way to go. The 7B bus, which permits you to take as much luggage as you can carry on your lap (not in the aisle), costs $1.15 (less for seniors and students). It leaves the Terminal at 1st & Mission from 5:30am-12:50am every quarter-hour, half-hour or hour, depending on the time of day. This bus can also be boarded at 3rd, 5th, 7th and 9th & Mission.

The 7F Express bus, which also permits only one carry-on piece of luggage, also costs $1.15 and makes the trip in about 36 minutes as compared to 55 minutes via the 7B. Phone 761-7000 for exact schedule for both buses.

Mini Buses to SF Airport

A number of small buses now provide service to and from the SF Airport; they all charge $7 per person and will pick you up at your hotel or home and drop you at your departing airline, or you can board them at the Airport and they will drop you off at your home or hotel. The first buses arrive at the Airport at about 6:15am and the last one leaves the Airport at about 10pm. You can find these buses in the upper level of the Airport, center traffic island, at the Courtesy Vehicle sign. They do not stop there, so you have to catch them on the run. Here they are, with phone numbers:

Airport Service, 552-4166.

California Minibus, 775-5121. Service every hour from 5:30am-10:30pm between S.F. Airport and downtown.

Downtown Airport Express, 775-5121.

Limousine Alternative, 397-5466. They use Lincoln town cars exclusively for door-to-door service from S.F. Airport to anywhere in the City. Fare to downtown is $25, to other areas $27-$30 for up to 4 passengers and luggage. These are basically taxi rates but with much more luxury.

The Lorrie Travel and Tour, 826-5950. This is the oldest service and very reliable.

Super Shuttle, 558-8500. The fastest-growing of the new services.

Yellow Airport and Tour Service, 262-7433.

Service to S.F. Airport, San Jose & Santa Clara

Francisco's Adventures. This 2-man firm has two Dodge vans which will take up to 1-6 persons for a total of $20 from S.F. to the Airport. Returning from the Airport, they cruise on the upper level and pick up passengers at the blue pillars. They will also take passengers from the SF Airport to San Jose for $12 a person, minimum 3 persons. For reservations phone 821-0903 or 824-0302.

AC Transit to Oakland Airport

To get to the Oakland Airport, take Bus N from the East Bay Terminal at 1st & Mission to Fruitvale & MacArthur Blvd stop, then transfer to a 57 bus to the Airport. Ride, including tranfer, costs $1.50 (seniors and students $0.70). The amount of luggage you can take is more or less up to the discretion of the bus driver but cannot exceed what you can carry, e.g., one large suitcase or 2 small bags. The N bus runs from 6:09am-12:23am. The entire trip, including the 57 bus, takes about an hour. The last bus leaves the Airport for S.F. at 12:47am. Phone 839-2882 for details.

BART to Oakland Airport

Take BART to the Coliseum Station in Oakland (Fremont Line) and transfer to the AIR-BART shuttle which runs every 10 minutes, 6am-midnight. The last bus returns from the Oakland Airport at 11:50pm. The transfer to the Shuttle costs $1.00. Phone 788-2278 for information.

Lorrie to Oakland Airport

Lorrie will pick you up and drive you and your luggage from San Francisco to the Oakland Airport for $34.75, 1-5 persons. Call at least 6 hours before flight time. Phone 826-5950.

Yellow Airport & Tour Service--to Oakland Airport

This mini-bus will take you from your home or hotel for $13.50 person, minimum 2. Phone 282-7433.

S.F. Airport to Oakland Airport

The Bay Area Bus Service runs buses from the San Francisco Airport to the Oakland Airport every 2 hours on the odd hour, from 7am-11pm and from Oakland Airport to S.F. Airport from 6am-10 pm. The fare is $7 per person either way. Phone 632-5506.

MUNI Buses, Street Cars, Metro

Adult fare is 75 cents, 15 cents for seniors over 65 and disabled persons, 25 cents for students 5-17, and free for children under 5. Monthly fast passes are $23 for adults, $5 for youths 5-17, $4.50 for seniors and disabled. Fast passes are good on all MUNI lines. Two transfers are free and can be used in all directions for the time shown (about 2 hours), except on cable cars (see below). Most buses run from 7am-1am but some run all night (Owl Service). Phone 673-6864 for information. Tell them where you are and where you want to go.

Other Transit

Cable Cars

Probably San Francisco's single most popular attraction, $1.50 for adults, 75 cents for youths 5-17, 15 cents for seniors over 65 and disabled persons, children under 5 free. An adult all-day pass for the whole MUNI system, including cable cars, is $5. A cable-car 30-ride booklet is $22.50 and is available at the Cable Car Museum, at MUNI headquarters (949 Presidio, Room 239), or at City Hall Information Booth. It is non-transferable and sold to San Francisco residents only, one book per month.

SamTrans

The San Mateo Transit buses run from downtown San Francisco to a number of cities along the Peninsula, e.g., San Mateo, Burlingame, Redwood City, San Carlos, as well as to the S.F. Airport (see above) and Daly City. For details and schedule phone 761-7000.

San Francisco-Larkspur Ferry

Used widely by residents of the two areas, this ferry is also a popular 50-minute tourist ride. It leaves the S.F. Ferry Terminal opposite the Embarcadero Center, which can be reached by MUNI or BART.

One-way adult fare is $2 on weekdays and $3 on weekends and holidays (seniors over 65 ride for half fare, children 12 and under ride free). Weekday service from San Francisco is from 9:45am-6:35pm (last ferry returns from Larkspur 5:35pm). On weekends and holidays service is from 11:50am-5:50pm (last ferry leaves Larkspur at 4:50pm). This ferry travels between Alcatraz and Treasure Island, past Angel Island and Tiburon. For information phone 332-6600.

Train Service

AMTRAK runs from the East Bay Terminal at 1st and Mission, via free bus to their Oakland station. From there you can go by train to points East and South, to Valley cities, national parks and clear across the country. Many Reno casinos run special trips at highly reduced fares and offer freebies. For information phone 982-8512.

The Southern Pacific Railway runs commuter trains many times daily between San Francisco and San Jose, as well as points in-between. For information phone 495-4546.

Car rentals

The airline terminals and downtown San Francisco (Hilton Hotel area and Mason Street) abound in rental offices. Information on car rentals can be found in the free tourist publications that are available at all large hotel lobbies; they often include discount coupons. Also, be sure to check the larger companies such as *Hertz* (433 Mason, phone 771-2200) for their weekly or weekend specials. Other companies worth trying: *Rent-A-Heap-Cheap*--777 Van Ness, 776-5450; *Rent-A-Junker*--Army at Valencia, 285-4545; *Rent-A-Wreck*--555 Ellis, 776-8700; *Run About Used Car Rentals*--682 Geary, 673-3448; *S.F. Economy Car Rental*--1540 Pine, 474-1155; *Alamo Rent-A-Car-*--656 Geary, 673-9696; *General Rent-A-Car*--124 Beacon Street, 952-4896 or 800-327-7607.

Most car rentals have limited mileage and require the cars to stay in the area. *Alamo* and *General* may offer unlimited mileage. If you plan to travel more than 100 miles per day and don't want to be keeled over by the cost, look for unlimited mileage deals only. Overseas travelers are advised to order rental cars from overseas since they can usually get unlimited mileage contracts and better rates.

Golden Gate Transit

This service runs to points across the Golden Gate Bridge, to Mt. Tamalpais, Stinson Beach and points en route. Phone 332-6600 for information on routes and prices.

Greyhound & Trailway Buses

These buses run to all parts of California and to much of the United States. They often advertise specials which they do not volunteer over the phone--ask. Phone 433-1500 for *Greyhound* and 982-6400 for *Trailways*. See telephone book for additional numbers.

City and Other Tours

A number of bus companies run City tours as well as tours to outlying areas of San Francisco, e.g., Sausalito, Muir Woods, Mt. Tamalpais, the Wine Country, Carmel, Monterey. Some are: *Lorries,* 826-5950; *Dolphin Tour Company,* 216 O'Farrell (Stockton), 441-6810; *Quality Tours,* 150 Powell Street, 788-6838; *Maxi-Tours,* 563-2151; *Great Pacific Tour Company,* 929-1700; *The Grand Tour Company (Gourmet Tours),* 654-8824 or 421-7477.

Excursions to Reno, Lake Tahoe and Las Vegas

A number of companies, including Greyhound, run bus trips--one day, overnight or 2 nights--to Lake Tahoe and Reno (some combine both cities) at very low rates. The one-day trip, from early morning until late evening, is about $25 and includes freebies, even cash when you arrive at the casinos. Their overnight trips are around $35-$38 and slightly more on a weekend or if you stay at a first-class hotel like the MGM or the Hilton. These trips are strictly promotional and are subsidized by the casinos who expect you to leave some cash there. But that is up to you. Food and drink are practically given away.

Some of the companies offering these trips are: *Hee Chan Tours,* 397-2830; *Lucky Reno Tours,* 864-2545; *Mr. T's Casino Tours,* 648-7970; *Betty's Tours,* 495-8430; *Plaza Casino Tours,* 421-3965. The *Hee Chan Tours* to Reno, with stay at the Hilton or MGM, is highly recommended. Consult the last pages of the *Sunday Examiner* pink section for advertisements of such tours.

The excursions to Las Vegas are usually in conjunction with a local airline and begin at about $129, including airfare and 1-2 night's lodging. Phone *Western Airlines* (800-862-0906) or *Air-Cal* (433-2660) for information. These are also advertised in the *Examiner's* Sunday pink section.

Alternative Bus Travel--Green Tortoise

This is an interesting and cheap means of transportation and holiday touring for "young" people from 15 to 75 who have a leisurely attitude toward life. The buses are stripped down, foam mattresses and overhanging bunks are added. There are 2 firm rules: no smoking and no shoes on the mattresses. The company has 8 buses and the owner, Gardner Kent, often drives one himself. *Green Tortoise* has trips every Friday and Monday to and from Los Angeles ($25 each way), and every Monday and Friday night to and from Seattle ($49 each way), as well as cross-country USA (S.F. to N.Y. or Boston) 10-day camping and cookout ($199 each way). There are weekend trips to Yosemite ($49 round trip) and a 9-day (Friday to Sunday) Grand Canyon Indian Country Tour from San Francisco for $199. They also have trips to Mexico, Alaska and other destinations on the same basis. Highly recommended for individualists and the adventuresome. Phone 285-2441 for schedules and rates.

Driveaway Cars

If you are prepared to deliver a car to another city and have a valid driver's license, good references and a minimum deposit ($75-$100), this is a good way to get there. The companies will usually supply a tankful of gas to distant locations. You pay for everything else, including road and bridge tolls. For very heavy cars you can negotiate more than a tankful. You can get from and to almost any large city, e.g., from New York City to San Francisco, if you shop around. Here are some companies in this area:

Auto Caravan, 1095 Market, Room 417, 864-8800.

American Auto Shippers, 1300 Bayshore Highway, Suite 199, Burlingame, CA 94010 (near the Airport), 342-9611.

Auto Driveaway Company, 83 Market, Suite 412, 777-3740.

Intercity Auto Hikers, 494 9th St. (Bryant), 434-6104.

IV. Lodging

San Francisco has the undeserved reputation of being one of the most expensive cities in the U.S. It gets this from business travelers who stay in the $100-$200 rooms in the large, deluxe hotels, also from travel agents who book their customers in hotels that pay them a commission. Once you know your way around, you'll find that hotels in San Francisco don't have to be expensive. San Francisco is over-built with hotels and is still building more.

Even in the high season you can get a first-class hotel room for, say, $50-$60 (double) that will compare favorably with the $100+ room your travel agent might recommend. You can also get a room with bath for around $35 (double), or a bed-and-breakfast room for less. Good, clean accomodations are also to be found in the $10-$15 category (per person, without tax), and even less. Prices are lower when there are 3 or 4 to a room. If possible, correspond in advance, especially in season, and reserve, enclosing one-night's deposit. Better, phone in advance and confirm availability or have a friend do so. Remember, almost all accomodations are quoted without tax (11%, except for private Bed-and-Breakfasts which are not taxed).

Hostels, Hostel-Type, $6-$10 Per Person

Hostels

SAN FRANCISCO INTERNATIONAL HOSTEL, (127 beds), Bldg 240, Fort Mason, 771-7277. Opens at 4:30pm daily. Hostel price is

$8 per night, no age limit, *3-day maximum stay*. To get there, take bus 30, 42, or 47 to Bay and Van Ness Avenue, walk one block on Bay to the entrance to Fort Mason. Restrictions: must be out of the room by

10am and out of the hostel from 2-4pm, and in by midnight (curfew). Advantages: cooking in communal kitchen, hike around piers, excellent site. For general information on hostels in the Marin Headlands, phone 331-2777 and Point Reyes, phone 663-8811.

To reserve a room by mail, send one night's deposit. Remember, maximum stay is 3 nights per 2-week period. If you are not a member and wish to become one, you can sign up when you show up the first time. A pass is $20 for ages 18-60 and $10 for 60 and over and under 18.

Hostel-Type Hotels

These are lodgings intended for young people. often dormitory-type. They are very simple but clean and adequate. Young people will often find the same spirit of cameraderie which they find in hostels.

EUROPEAN GUEST HOUSE (15 rooms), 763 Minna (between 8th and 9th, just south of Mission), 861-6634. $6.50 per night per person, dormitory style, 3-6 in a room. Communal kitchen, social room with TV, showers. Has large European clientele. They organize wine-country trips, beach parties, and serve as communications center for youth travel. Well-located, near Holiday-Inn and the Greyhound bus terminal. Just off the Tenderloin, patronized by men and women. **(7)

YOUTH HOSTEL CENTRALE (24 rooms), 116 Turk (Taylor), 346-7835. There are 2 bunks in a room. Single $19, double $22. Located 2 blocks from the Airporter Terminal and Hilton. Hotel is clean and they run a "tight ship". Tenderloin area but busy and relatively safe. ***(7)

THE INTERNATIONAL TRAVELERS' NETWORK. locations: THE ELLIS COTEL (15 rooms), 222 Ellis (Mason), 441-8454; MISSION COTEL (30 rooms), 1906 Mission (15 St), St.), 441-8454. $10 per person per night, 2 to a room. *This price includes tax, bedding, shower etc.* Recreation room, reading room, no curfew. Information on travel, flights etc. Mostly foreign travelers, both sexes. Clean, well-run facilities at low price, without frills. ****BEST BUY (1)(16)

UNIVERSITY OF CALIFORNIA, S.F., Housing Office, 510 Parnassus, 476-5997. Dormitory housing during summer months only. Pool, gym. ****BEST BUY(18)

SAN FRANCISCO STATE U., Housing Office, 800 Font Blvd, 469-1067. Twin-bedded room with share bath and dormitory housing for students during summer months. **** BEST BUY(18)

Y's

YWCA (32 rooms, 1/2 with bath), 620 Sutter (Mason/Taylor), 775-6500. For women, also for men if accompanied by a woman. Prices for members--single without bath $24, with private bath $28; double without bath $34, with bath $38. Room for 3 with bath $48. Pool is open 6am-9pm. Prices for non-members are considerably higher but membership can be obtained onthe-spot for $25. Facilities include pool, gym, jacuzzi, sauna and weight room. Reservations, well in advance, are a must. Hotel is being totally renovated during first half of 1987. ****BEST BUY(1)

EMBARCADERO YMCA CENTER (269 rooms, showers in hall), 166 The Embarcadero, 392-2191. For men and women, no age restrictions. The use of the athletic facilities is included in the room rate. Singles $21.25 ($23.25 with color TV). Bunk beds for 2 in a room, $30.50 for 2, with TV $32.50. The rooms on the freeway side can be noisy but have an interesting Bay view. No membership required. ***(8)

YMCA CENTRAL BRANCH (109 rooms), 220 Golden Gate (Hyde), 885-0460. For men and women. Rates include tax. Rates also include use of pool and gym facilities. Singles without bath $24.71, doubles without bath $32.51. Single with bath $28.30. No membership required. ***(9)

YMCA CHINATOWN (47 rooms), 855 Sacramento (Stockton), 982-4412. Men only, 16 and older. Rates include tax, also use of pool, gym, and weight room. Single without bath $18, double $25. Weekly--single $100, double $140. No membership required. ***(2)

Economical Hotels, $10-$20 Per Person

This listing is based on the lowest rate per person for double occupancy without tax (11%). An adjustment of $2 is made when breakfast is included in the rate.

BEST BUY****

OLYMPIC HOTEL (85 rooms, 1/2 with bath), 140 Mason (Ellis), 982-5010. Single without bath $20, double without bath $25; single or double with bath $35, twins with bath, shower and TV $40. These rates *include* tax of 11%. This hotel is used by German and other tour groups. It is right next to the new Ramada Renaissance, across from the Hilton. Clean and well-run, extremely good value. ****BEST BUY (1)

MARINE MEMORIAL CLUB (143 rooms, most with bath), 609 Sutter (Taylor), 673-6672. Membership $60 1st year, $50 each year thereafter--is available for anyone who has served in the U.S. armed forces and their children over 21 years of age. Single $40-55, double $45-$60, guests $10 extra. Rooms without bath $20. ****BEST BUY(1)

ADELAIDE INN (16 rooms, hall baths), 5 Adelaide Place (off Taylor, near Post), 441-2261. *Rates include hot rolls and coffee for breakfast.* Single $28, double or twin beds $38. A kitchenette and microwave are available for light food preparation, e.g. sandwiches, salads, soups. Charming character. ****BEST BUY (1)

ANSONIA HOTEL AND RESIDENCE CLUB, 711 Post St. (Jones), 673-2670. Men & women, age 18-35. Single from $30, double from $36. Weekly: $100-$160. *Includes expanded complimentary breakfast Mon-Sat.* Popular with American & foreign students. ****BEST BUY(1)

GEARY HOTEL (120 rooms, 100 with bath), 610 Geary (Jones/Leavenworth), 673-9221. Single without bath $22, double $24; single with bath $32, double $35-$38, twin beds $42-$48, 3-4 persons $45. Students receive $3 discount. European style, very popular. ****BEST BUY(1)

PENSION INTERNATIONAL (49 rooms, 12 with bath), 875 Post (Hyde/ Leavenworth), 775-3344. *Rates include continental breakfast.* Single without bath $18-$25, double $25-$35 (price depends on size of room and season). Single with bath $30-$40, double $40-$50. Weekly--single without bath $90-$120, double $135-$160; single with bath $155-$190, double $175-$225. Older but well-kept building & facilities. ****BEST BUY(1)

THE AMSTERDAM HOTEL (26 rooms, most with bath), 749 Taylor (Sutter) 673-3277. Old world charm, old-fashioned looking, clean.

Single without bath $32, double $37. Single with bath $45, double $48, 3 in a room $53, 4 in a room $58. Complimentary coffee in lobby at all times. Hotel was completely renovated in 1983. ****BEST BUY(1)

CAMBRIDGE HOTEL (65 rooms, all with bath, color TV), 473 Ellis (Leavenworth/Jones), 673-7232. Renovated in 1986. Clean, well-run. Single $25-$38, double $29-$38, triple $45. Low-priced parking available. ****BEST BUY(9)

TEMPLE HOTEL (120 rooms, 20 with bath), 469 Pine (Kearny/Montgomery), 781-2565. Single without bath $22, double $25, roll-away $5 extra. Single with bath $27, double $30, triple $37. Weekly rates: single without bath $84 (incl. tax), double $98 plus tax); single with bath $98, double $112, both including tax. This is a clean, well-run hotel, in the heart of the business area, not too far from the East Bay Terminal at 1st & Mission. ****BEST BUY(8).

SEQUOIA HOTEL, 520 Jones (O'Farrell), 441-9710. Hotel was largely destroyed by fire but is now being completely rebuilt. Phone for rates. It will probably remain in the BEST BUY category. (9)

ATHERTON HOTEL (80 rooms, 70 with bath), 685 Ellis (Larkin), 474-5720. Single or double $34-$65, extra bed $6. The 6 rooms without bath are in a house across the street and are rented by the week only for $147-$161. ****BEST BUY(9)

ESSEX HOTEL (105 rooms, 56 with bath), 684 Ellis (Larkin), 474-4664. Single without bath $30, double $34; single with bath $38, double $44-$48; suites for 3-4, 2 rooms, $71. ****BEST BUY(9)

OBRERO HOTEL & BASQUE RESTAURANT (12 rooms, hall baths), 1208 Stockton (Pacific), 989-3960. *Rates include a huge break-fast consisting of fruit, egg, ham, cheese, hot sourdough bread, honey, jam, coffee or tea .* Single $35, double $42, triple $57. Altogether, an excellent value. This hotel is located in the heart of Chinatown shopping area and also has an interesting Basque restaurant. A 7-course meal with *t wo* entrees, including soup, salad, wine, dessert and coffee is $10.50 plus tax and tip. See under Basque Restaurants. ****BEST BUY(2)

GRANT HOTEL (76 rooms, all with bath, shower, TV), 753 Bush (Powell), 421-7540. Single $35, double $40, extra person $5. Hotel is older but clean, refurbished in 1984. Two blocks north of Union Square, safe area. ****BEST BUY(2)

GRANT PLAZA (72 rooms with bath, color TV, phone), 465 Grant Avenue (Pine). 434-3883. Single $27, double $32, twin beds $37, family suite, up to 5 persons, $72. Hotel was renovated in 1985. Rooms are small but clean and comfortable. ****BEST BUY(2)

BUDGET INN (23 rooms, all with bath), 111 Bade St. (Gough/Bade, near Market), 626-4155. Single $36, double $38. ****BEST BUY(10)

PENSION SAN FRANCISCO (32 rooms, 16 hall baths), 1668 Market (Van Ness and Haight), 864-1271. *Rates include capuccino or espresso in the morning.* Single $32, double $38, twin beds $41, suite (2 rooms) $70 for 2, futon for 3rd person $5. Restaurant (Pension Cafe) and wine bar on premises. Charming, very popular. ****BEST BUY(15)

GOUGH-HAYES HOTEL (70 rooms, hall baths), 417 Gough (Hayes), 431-9131. Hotel has 7 kitchens for sharing. Single $11-$30 (depending on size and location), double $25-33. Weekly rates--single $75-$150, double $110-$70. Hotel consists of four 3-story Victorians, most rooms are furnished with antiques. Facilities: sauna and gym, washer and dryer, color TV, BBQ patio, sundeck. Hotel is gay-oriented. ****BEST BUY(10)

GOTHAM HOTEL (114 rooms, all with bath), 835 Turk (Franklin), 928-7291. Weekly rates only--single $100, double $110-$120. Rooms are simple but clean. The hotel was refurbished in 1986. ****BEST BUY (10)

SAN REMO HOTEL (62 rooms, hall baths), 2237 Mason (Francisco/Chestnut), 776-8688. May-October--single $35, double $50, triple $60. October-May weekly only $100-$125. Probably the cheapest rates for the Fisherman's Wharf area. ****BEST BUY(4)

THE GROVE INN (18 rooms, 5 with bath), 890 Grove Street (Fillmore), 929-0780. *Rates include complimentary continental breakfast.* Single, shared bath $35, suite, 2 rooms, up to 4 persons, with private bath $55, extra person $5. Off-street parking available, $2 per day. Weekly rates on request. This is an extremely well-run hotel. The immediate area is safe but at night the approach--especially via the 22 Fillmore bus--calls for caution. ****BEST BUY(14)

METRO HOTEL (22 rooms, all with bath, color TV), 319 Divisadero (Page/Oak), 861-5634. Single $25, double $35, twin beds $45, 2 double beds (up to 4 persons) $49. Victoria style, European character.

Neighborhood is mixed but safe, 2 blocks from Haight. Hotel was remodeled in 1984. ****BEST BUY(14)

EDWARD II (30 rooms), corner Scott and Lombard, 921-9776. *Rates include continental breakfast.* Single (3 rooms only) $35 without bath, double without bath $42.50. Double with bath $55, with 2 double beds $65, extra persons $7 each. In-out parking $6 per day. Neighborhood location, charming pension atmosphere but a bit loud on the Lombard side. ****BEST BUY(6)

THE RED VICTORIAN (16 rooms, 3 with bath), 1665 Haight (Cole/ Belvedere), 864-1978. *Rates include continental breakfast.* Single without bath $35-$55, double $40-$45; single or double with bath $67-$74, additional person $10. Near Golden Gate Park, in the heart of the Haight-Ashbury scene. ****BEST BUY(14)

DIAMOND HOUSE (3 rooms, hall bath, deck), Diamond & 18th Sts $45-$55 double. *Rates include an American breakfast.* Facilities include a hot tub and gazebo. ****BEST BUY (15)

SIMPLE(*)--VERY GOOD(***)

HILL POINT GUEST HOUSES (10 guest homes in the area, 42 rooms, some with bath), 15 Hillpoint Ave. (Parnassus Ave/Irving), 753-0393. Caters to students and guests visiting nearby University of California Medical Center on Parnassus Avenue. Single $20 daily, $120 weekly, double $25 daily, $150 weekly. Rooms with bath higher. Shared kitchen facilities, coin-operated laundry room. ****BEST BUY(18)

SIMPLE(*) TO VERY GOOD(***)

Listed roughly in order of distance from Union Square.

STRATFORD HOTEL (105 rooms, 55 with bath), 242 Powell (Union Square), 421-7525. Single without bath $15, double $20. Single with bath $27.50, double $32.50. Rollaway +$5. In process of refurbishing, should be finished by mid-1987. Excellent location but rooms facing street are loud. ***(1)

ALL SEASON'S HOTEL (89 rooms, about half with bath), 417 Stockton (Union Square), 986-8737. *Rates include continental breakfast.* Single without bath $32, double $35, twin beds $39. triple $46, quad $50. ***(1)

WILL ROGERS HOTEL (91 rooms, 32 with bath) 589 Post (Mason/Taylor), 441-9378. By the week only--single without bath $60, single or double with bath $90. ***(1)

VIRGINIA HOTEL (120 rooms, some 50 with bath), 312 Mason (O'Farrell), 673-9600. Single without bath $30, double $35; single with bath $35, double $40. About half the rooms have color TV. Hotel is old but well-kept. Good location near Union Square. ***(1)

WINDSOR HOTEL (125 rooms, 1/2 with bath), 238 Eddy (Taylor/Jones, just behind the Airporter Terminal), 885-0101. Prices are the same as the Olympic Hotel, same management--see BEST BUYS--but I rate this slightly lower because it is in a run-down area. ***(7)

HOTEL GATES (144 rooms, 1/2 with baths), 140 Ellis (Mason), 781-0430. Single without bath $22, double $25; single with bath $24, double $30, extra person $2.50. **(9)

HYDE PLAZA (51 rooms, 4 with bath), 835 Hyde (Bush/Sutter) 885-2987. Weekly and monthly only. Single without bath $80 weekly, $300-$540 monthly; double $95-$110 and $340-$600, respectively. **(1)

GOLDEN GATE HOTEL (30 rooms, 12 with private bath), 775 Bush/Powell), 392-3702. Single or double without bath $39, single or double with bath $54. 2 blocks from Union Square. **(1).

GRAND CENTRAL HOTEL (100 rooms, 10 with bath) 1412 Market (10th St.),431-9190. Single without bath $20, by week $80. Double without bath $28 by week $120 (also twin). Single with bath $30, double $34. A few rooms with bath and 2 double beds--$29, for 3 $37, for 4 $40. Entrance is shabby but rooms are clean. **(7)

HOTEL GAYLORD (156 rooms with kitchenettes), 620 Jones (Geary/ Post), 673-8445. Single $135 week, $540 month; double 150 week, $575 month. **(1)

HOTEL EMBASSY (80 rooms, all with bath & color TV), 610 Polk (Turk), 673-1404. Single $39, double $40, 2 beds $46. ***(9)

LELAND HOTEL (107 rooms, 80 with bath), 1315 Polk (Bush), 441-5141. Single or double without bath $25-$30; single with bath $35, double $44. Weekly--single without bath $90-$110,, with bath $130; double with bath $150. Bus to Airport $5. Hotel is gay-oriented. ***(10)

CABLE CAR HOTEL (69 rooms, hall baths), 1385 California (Hyde), 441-9857. Weekly rates only--single $80-$90, double $100. ***(1)

CHARLIE'S HOTEL (16 rooms, all with bath and color TV), 1030 Geary (Van Ness), 673-3906. Single $33, double $39, triple $45, quad $50. ***(1)

SHANGRI-LA INN HOTEL (30 rooms, all with bath, color TV), 1356 Van Ness (Bush), 776-9300. *Rates include continental breakfast.* Single $35, double $40, twin beds $45; 3-4 persons, 2 double beds, $49. ***(10)

HOTEL EUROPA (79 rooms, all without bath), 310 Columbus (Broadway), 391-5779. Single $20, double $25, 3 persons (double plus 2 single beds) $30 per day; 4 persons (double beds) $44. Single $80 week, double $93. Some renovation in 1984. **(3)

HOTEL CHIPPENDALE (17 rooms, 2 hall baths), 492 Grove (Octavia), 861-8686. This is a gayoriented hotel. Rates by the week and for singles only--$65-$100. Has communal kitchen, parlor with color TV. Rooms have individual gas heat. A laundromat is just around the corner. Completely refurbished in 1984-85. ***(10)

ECONO INN MOTEL (37 rooms, all with bath, color TV), 2322 Lombard (Pierce/Scott), 921-4980. Single $34, double $38. Free parking. All rooms refurbished in 1986. ***(6)

JACK'S HOUSE (5 rooms, hall bath), 311 Steiner (Haight), 863-0947. Single $20, double $30. Large, clean rooms, use of community kitchen (utensils, condiments supplied free), garden for sunning, information center, group discussions, family atmosphere. Rates are high for rooms without private bath but worth it for those who wish to explore the Haight-Ashbury scene. The neighborhood is safe but the approach is questionable, although several buses (Nos. 6,7,66,71) run right to the door. ***(14)

Intermediate Hotels, $20-$30 Per Person

This listing is based on the lowest rate per person for double occupancy, without tax (11%). An adjustment of $2 is made when breakfast is included in the rate.

Unless otherwise noted, all rooms in the following hotels have private baths, color TVs and inroom phones. Listed in order of distance from Union Square.

BEST BUY****

ALEXANDER HOTEL (75 rooms, 67 with bath), 415 O'Farrell (Taylor), 928-6800. Single without bath $29, with bath $39, double with bath $44; suite, 2 connecting rooms and bath, for 3 $68, for 4 $78. Hotel was refurbished completely in 1986. ****BEST BUY(9)

MOSSER VICTORIAN (166 rooms), 54 4th St. (Market/Mission), 986-4400 or 800-227-3804 in California. Single $32, double $42-$49. ****BEST BUY(7)

MARK TWAIN (115 rooms), 345 Taylor (O'Farrell/Ellis), 673-2332. Single $48, double $59, twin beds $61, triple add $12. ****BEST BUY(9)

BERESFORD ARMS (95 rooms, half with kitchenette), 701 Post (Jones), 673-2600. *Rates include free donuts and coffee for breakfast.* Single $55, double $55. Room with kitchenette, double, $75-$95, each additional person $5. Elegant hotel, probably the best buy in all of San Francisco in terms of price, comfort, decor. ****BEST BUY(1)

OXFORD HOTEL (115 rooms), Market at Mason), 775-4600. *Rates include continental breakfast.* Single $39, double $45, triple $51, 2 double beds, up to 4 persons, $57. In-out parking $6.50 per day. ****BEST BUY(7)

EL CORTEZ (170 rooms, 90% with kitchenette) 550 Geary (Taylor/Jones), 775-5000. Single $50, double $56, 3 persons $60, 4 persons $65. ****BEST BUY(1)

HOTEL SAVOY (83 rooms), 580 Geary (Taylor/Jones), 441-2700 or 800-622-0553 in California. Single $58-$68, double $68-$78. ****BEST BUY(1)

BERESFORD HOTEL (112 rooms), 635 Sutter (Mason), 673-9900. Single $55, double $56, triple $60, quad $65. ****BEST BUY(1)

UN PLAZA (135 rooms), Market at 7th, 626-5200. *Rates include continental breakfast.* Single $39, double $45. In-out parking $7.50 daily. Same management as the Oxford Hotel. ****BEST BUY

CORNELL HOTEL (58 rooms, 40 with bath), 715 Bush (Stockton), 421-3154. French management, large French clientele. Single without bath $35, with bath $45, double with bath $50. Weekly rates, *including breakfast and dinner,* 5 days--single with bath $265, double $315. Monthly rate, single, $750. Food is prepared by professional cooks who used to run the restaurant on the premises (Jeanne d'Arc) which has closed down but which will probably open again by the time this edition appears. ****BEST BUY(1)

CANTERBURY HOTEL (250 rooms), 750 Sutter (Taylor/Jones), 474-6464 or 800-227-4788. Single $52, double $59, extra bed $10. ****BEST BUY(1)

STANYAN PARK HOTEL (36 rooms), 750 Stanyan (Walnut), 751-1000. *Rates include continental breakfast.* Single or double $58-$68, extra person $20. In-out parking in the area $1.50 day. ****BEST BUY(14)

THE MONTE CRISTO (14 rooms, 12 with bath), 600 Presidio Avenue (Pine), 931-1875. *Rates include expanded continental breakfast.* Single or double, shared bath, $50-$55, private bath $65-$95. All rooms are decorated in antiques. ****BEST BUY(11)

WILLOWS INN (11 rooms, shared baths), 710 14th St. (Market/Church), 431-4770. *Rates include breakfast consisting of freshly-squeezed orange juice, croissant & coffee.* Single $50-$72, double $55-$82 (prices depend on size of room and whether double or queen-size beds). Suite of 2 rooms, $90 for 2 persons, $110 for 3-4. Furniture is Gypsy-Willows (hence, the name) and the decor Laura Ashley. Excellent French restaurant (Piano Zinc) is on ground floor. ****BEST BUY(15)

CASTRO HOTEL (6 2-room suites with bath), 560 Castro (18/19 Sts), 621-6222. Single $55, double $60. Elegant Victorian residence, fireplaces, view of Twin Peaks. Gay-oriented. **** BEST BUY(15)

GOOD(*) TO VERY GOOD(***)

CONTINENTAL HOTEL (100 rooms), Cyril Magnin Street (5th at Ellis), 982-3772. Closed for remodeling as edition went to press but may be open by the beginning of the 1987 season and may well be a BEST BUY then. (9)

HOTEL MERLIN (189 rooms), 5th & Mission, 4217500. Single $50, double $60, 3 in room $70. Free HBO. ****BEST BUY(7)

MAYFLOWER HOTEL APTS (100 rooms, with kitchenette), 975 Bush (Jones), 673-7010. Single $40 daily, $240 weekly, $675 monthly; double $50 daily, $300 weekly, $875 monthly. ***(1)

COMMODORE HOTEL (113 rooms), 825 Sutter (Jones), 885-2464. Single $40-$50, double $45-$65, extra person $10. ***(1)

HOTEL BRITTON (79 rooms), 112 7th St. (Mission/Market), 621-7001. Jan 1-22 May--single $44-$49, double $51-$57. From 23 May--single $47-$52, double $54-$62. ***(7)

CASA ARGUELLO (6 units, 3 with bath), 225 Arguello Blvd (California/ Sacramento), 752-482. *Rates include continental breakfast.* Single or double, shared bath, $43, double with private bath $48-$58, apartment for 2 or 3 $58-$68, 2 room suite with bath, for 4, $78. In residential area with good bus transportation to downtown (15-20 minutes). ****BEST BUY(22)

ROBERTS AT THE BEACH (30 rooms), 2828 Sloat Blvd (46 St), 564-2610. Single $42, double $45, double with 2 beds $52, additional occupant $5. A street car to Market Street stops at the door, 30-35 minutes to downtown. ****BEST BUY(20)

Motels

The following motels are listed in order of distance from Union Square. Unless otherwise noted, all have private baths, color TV, free parking.

BEST BUY****

COMFORT INN (67 rooms), 240 7th St.(Howard/Folsom), 861-6469 or 800-228-5150. *Rates include continental breakfast and use of sauna.* Single $48, double $54, 2 double beds for up to 4 persons $65. Mini suites, 1 bedroom 1 sitting, up to 4 persons $65. $10 surcharge Friday or Saturday. ****BEST BUY(7)

DOWNTOWN MOTEL (23 rooms), 111 Page (Gough), 626-4155. Single $34, double $38, 2 beds $42. Near Opera, Davies Hall etc. Free covered parking. Remodeled in 1985. ****BEST BUY(10)

RODEWAY INN (73 rooms), 895 Geary (Larkin), 441-8220 or 800-228-2000. Single $50, double $58, extra person $6. Two-room suite for 2 $63, extra person $6. ****BEST BUY(1)

BENTLEY MOTOR INN (39 rooms), 465 Grove (Octavia), 864-4040. Single $38, double $42, triple $50, quad $52, 2-room suite, up to 4 persons, $58. Refurbished 1986. ****BEST BUY(10)

PACIFIC HEIGHTS INN (40 rooms), 1555 Union (Van Ness/Franklin), 776-3310. *Rates include continental breakfast.* Single or double $55, 2 beds $65, double with steam room or jacuzzi $60-$65, 2-room suite for 2-3 $60-$70. Family-run, clean. ****BEST BUY(5)

MARINA MOTEL (44 rooms, 18 with kitchenette), 2576 Lombard Broderick/Divisadero), 921-9406. Single-double $33.50, twin $35.50 2 double beds, for 4, $45.50. Free parking. ****BEST BUY(6)

ALFA INN MOTEL, corner Divisadero & Lombard (28 rooms, 22 with kitchenette, all with bath & color TV), 921-3505. Single or double $40, queen bed with kitchen $44; 2 queens and kitchen, for up to 4 persons, $46; 2 queens and single, for up to 5, $59. Free HBO. ****BEST BUY(6)

VERY GOOD***

FLAMINGO MOTOR INN BEST WESTERN, (38 rooms), 114 - 7th St. (Howard/Folsom). Single $48-$56, double $53-$63, extra person $7. ***(7)

THE RED COACH (45 rooms), 825 Polk (Ellis), 771-2199 (Polk/Eddy). Single $45, double $48, triple $52, quad $55. ***(10)

CIVIC MANOR MOTEL (29 rooms), 825 Polk (Ellis), 673-0411. Single $6, double $50. ***(10)

TRAVELODGE CIVIC CENTER (80 rooms), 790 Ellis (Polk), 775-7612. *Rates include continental breakfast*. Single $47, double $52-$62, extra person $5. ***(10)

GARDEN INN (44 rooms), 601 Eddy (Larkin), 776-1380. Has outdoor heated pool. Single $45, double $50, suite for 2 $75. Extra person in double or suite $10. ***(9)

TRAVEL LOUNGE MOTOR HOTEL CIVIC CENTER (100 rooms), 655 Ellis (Polk), 771-3000 or 800-223-9889 within California. Single $39-$54, double $45-$64, extra person $5. Covered parking. ***(9)

VAN NESS MOTEL (42 rooms), 2850 Van Ness Ave., (Lombard/Chestnut), 776-3220. Single or double $36. ***(10)

BECKS'S MOTOR LODGE (57 rooms), 2222 Market (15 St), 621-8212 or 800-622-0797 in California. Single $45-$50, double $50-$55, extra person $4. ***(15)

LOMBARD PLAZA MOTEL (32 rooms), 2026 Lombard (Webster-Fillmore), 921-2444. Single $39, double $41, extra person $5. ***(6)

MANOR MOTEL (32 rooms), 2358 Lombard (Pierce/Scott), 922-2010. Single $42, double $44, extra person $5. ***(6)

GEARY PARKWAY MOTEL, (20 rooms, all with bath, color TV), 4750 Geary Blvd (12 Av), 752-4406. Single or double $39; 2 double beds, for up to 4, $49. *Complimentary coffee in room.* ***(13)

SUNSET MOTEL (10 rooms), 821 Taraval (off Highway 1, between 18th & 19th Avs), 564-3656. Single $34, double $37, 3-4 persons $47. ***(19)

OCEANVIEW MOTEL (23 rooms, all with bath, color TV), 4340 Judah (Great Highway, Pacific beach), 661-2300. Single or double $32, triple $42. Free parking. ***(23)

Splurge Hotels, $30-$40 Per Person

Based on the lowest rate per person for double occupancy, without tax (11%). Unless otherwise indicated, all listings include private bath, color TV and room phone. Listed roughly in order of distance to Union Square.

BEST BUY****

CHANCELLOR HOTEL (148 rooms), 433 Powell (facing Union Square), 362-2004. This hotel recently received a $2.3 million face-lift which included double-paned windows. Single $65, double $70, twin $75, extra person $10. ****BEST BUY(1)

HOTEL CECIL (150 rooms), 545 Post (Powell), 673-3733. Single $52, double $65, extra person $10; 2-room suite for 3-4 $110. ****BEST BUY(1)

POWELL HOTEL (165 rooms), 17 Powell (Market), 398-3200. Single $55, double $65. At the foot of Market, opposite the cable-car turntable, right in the heart of things. ****BEST BUY(1)

KING GEORGE HOTEL, (144 rooms), 334 Mason (Geary/ O'Farrell), 781-5050. Single $65, double $69. Seniors are given 10% discount or continental-buffet breakfast. An innovative 2-night package deal for 2, "Union Square Delight",--$46 per person per night, double occupancy. Includes theater ticket, 2 continental breakfasts, an afternoon High Tea with classical music and many freebies & discounts in the Union Square area. Another 2-night package "Gourmet Getaway"--includes an afternoon High Tea, a dinner at a French restaurant ($20 voucher per person), and a dinner at a Japanese restaurant ($10 voucher per person)--$51.75 per person per night, double occupancy. Also, an elaborate High Tea, $8.50. Hotel is being completely renovated in 1987. ****BEST BUY(9)

THE ANDREWS HOTEL (48 rooms), 624 Post (Taylor), 563-6877 or 800-622-0557 in California. *Rates include continental breakfast and wine in the afternoon.* Single or double $66-$96, extra person $8. ****BEST BUY(1)

EMPEROR NORTON INN (10 rooms, 1 suite), 615 Post (Taylor/
Mason), 775-2567. *Rates include complimentary breakfast and bottle
of wine.* Single or double without bath $75, suite (living room, bed-
room, kitchen, bath) $110. Handcrafted furniture, turn-of-century
decor. ****BEST BUY(1)

WHITEHALL INN (40 rooms), 750 Sutter (Taylor), 474-6464 or
800- 652-1614 in California. Same management as Hotel Canterbury
next door. Single $62, double $69. ****BEST BUY(1)

ABIGAIL HOTEL (60 rooms), 246 McAllister (Larkin/Hyde), 861-
9278. Single $55, double $65, extra person $8. Full bar and restaurant
on premises. Charming Victorian decor (antiques), a bit of England in
San Francisco, popular with opera and theater artists. ****BEST
BUY(9)

ARGYLE HOTEL (61 rooms, all with kitchen), 146 McAllister
(Leavenworth/Hyde), 552-7076. Single $55, double $65, extra person
$10. Weekly rates--single $325, double $375. Charming ambience,
popular with theater and opera artists. Complimentary coffee in
lobby. ****BEST BUY(9)

BEVERLY PLAZA (150 rooms), 342 Grant (Bush, at gate to Chinatown), 781-3566 or 800-227-3818 in California. Single $54-$60,
double $62-$66, extra bed $6. In-out parking $5 day. Renovated in
1986. ****BEST BUY(2)

LOMBARD HOTEL (102 rooms), 1015 Geary (Polk/Van Ness),
673-5232. Single or double $66, extra person $10. *Complimentary
tea or sherry 5:30-6:30 pm, wine and cheese party every Thursday.*
****BEST BUY(9)

INN SAN FRANCISCO (15 rooms, 11 with bath), 943 South Van
Ness (20/21 Sts), 641-0188. *Rates include buffet breakfast, use of hot
tub, sun deck & gardens.* Double with shared bath $52, queen bed
with shared bath $66. Double with private bath $76-$98 (price de-
pends on size, location, furnishings). Garden-view rooms with spa-
tub for 2, fireplace or private balcony $120-$149. Garage parking $5.
For those who can afford it, this is an unusual Inn, beautifully restored in Victorian decor, with luxurious amenities and personal service. ****BEST BUY(16)

VERY GOOD

HOTEL DAVID (50 rooms, some without bath), 480 Geary (Mason/Taylor), 771-1600. *Rates include full breakfast, 10% discount on prices in restaurant, and free transportation from S.F. Airport.* Single without bath $58, with bath $69, double with bath $79; 2 doubles without bath $64; 2 connecting rooms with bath, up to 4 persons, $116. ***(1)

REDWOOD INN (312 rooms), 1530 Lombard (Franklin), 776-3800. *Rates include continental breakfast, free parking.* Single $65, double $70, triple $80. ***(6)

CARLTON HOTEL (160 rooms), 107 Sutter (Larkin), 673-0242. Single $58, double $68, triple $80. Inout parking $6.50. Good, low-priced restaurant on premises. ***(1)

VAGABOND INN (135 rooms), 2550 Van Ness (Filbert), 776-7500. *Rates include HBO and Showtime movies, coffee and tea in lobby, apples (the eating kind), free parking.* Single $54, double $65, extra person $6. Discount for AAA members. ***(10)

LAUREL MOTOR INN (49 rooms, 18 with kitchenette), Corner Presidio and California, 567-8467. *Rates include continental breakfast, free parking.* Single $59-$67, double $66-$71. Higher prices are for city-view rooms. Free van shuttle service to major hospitals. ***(11)

Big Splurge, $40-$50 Per Person

This is for double occupancy, excluding tax (11%). As explained in the Introduction, this category is for the one-time special occasion, or for well-heeled travelers. These accomodations rival the deluxe hotels who charge up to $200. What has made this possible is the unusual number of expensive renovations of larger, older hotels, each at at a cost of as much as $7 million. They now serve as a good alternative to the deluxe hotels which charge $150-$200 for a double and which only the rich or those on a good expense-account can afford. Most of these remodeled hotels have rates just under $100, making them just right for my *Big Splurge*. Thus, all hotels in this category are considered ****BEST BUY. Look especially at those hotels that offer complimentary breakfast (some offer tea or wine in the afternoon as well), as this is a great luxury when travelling.

VILLA FLORENCE (177 rooms), 225 Powell (Geary/O'Farrell), 397-7700 or 800-243-5700. This was the old Manx hotel which was face-lifted at a cost of some millions. *Rates include complimentary wine in evenings by the wood-burning fireplace.* Single or double $89, Junior Suites $99, Deluxe Suites $149, up to 4-5 persons. Close to Union Square, Market St., cable car. ****BEST BUY(9)

KENSINGTON PARK HOTEL (96 rooms), 450 Post (Powell/Stockton), facing Union Square), 788-6400 or 800-553-1900. This is the old Elks Lodge hotel which was renovated for $7 million in 1984 just before the Democratic Convention. *Rates include coffee and croissants in the morning, tea and sherry in the afternoon, newspaper each morning.* Single or double $95-$105. The upper corner rooms have stunning views of Nob Hill and Union Square at no extra price. ****BEST BUY(1)

HOTEL UNION SQUARE (131 rooms), 114 Powell (Ellis), 397-3000 or 800-583-1900. Renovated in 1982 for some $4 million. Some rooms are rather small. *Rates include continental breakfast.* Single or double $65-$95, extra person $10. ****BEST BUY(9)

HOTEL DIVA (100 rooms), 440 Geary Mason/Taylor), 864-1876 or 800-553-1900. This 1912 building was renovated at a cost of some millions in a combination of modern and baroque. *Rates include continental breakfast.* Single or double $90, double-double $100 (up to 4 persons). One block from Union Square and cable car. Brand new, deluxe accomodations. VCR in every room. ****BEST BUY(1)

HOTEL RAPHAEL (151 rooms), 386 Geary (Mason/Powell), 986-2000 or 800-821-5343. Single $72, double $85. Extra person $10. One block from Union Square, often called the "Poor Man's St. Francis". An elegant alternative. ****BEST BUY(1)

ORCHARD HOTEL (96 rooms), 562 Sutter (Mason/Powell), 433-4434 or 800-433-4343). This is part of a prestigious chain which has hotels in Australia and Singapore. Hotel was opened in 1985 and shows Asian influence, including oriental prints in rooms. Single or double $85-$105, extra person $10. ****BEST BUY(1)

VINTAGE COURT (106 rooms), 650 Bush (Powell), 392-4666 or 800-654-7266. *Rates include complimentary wine in the afternoon.* Single or double $84, extra person $10. ****BEST BUY(1)

JULIANA (107 rooms), 590 Bush (Stockton), 392-2540 or 800-372-8800. *Rates include continental breakfast and wine in the afternoon.* Single or double $89. One block to Union Square. ****BEST BUY(1)

EXECUTIVE SUITES (41 suites), 567-5151 (reservations). Suite locations: 725 Pine, Hyde & Larkin, Franklin & Eddy, Greenwich & Van Ness, 3rd & Folsom (Moscone Center). Studio, for 1 or 2, $75-80 daily; 1 bed with living-dining and kitchen $85-100 for 2 (extra bed $50 week); 2 bedrooms, 2 baths, living-dining, kitchen $110-$130 daily. Maid service Mon-Fri. ****BEST BUY(1)

GALLERIA PARK (177 rooms) 191 Sutter (Kearny), 781-3060 or 800-792-9639. This is a multi-million dollar renovation of the Sutter Hotel, in 1984. Single or double $95, no extra charge for extra person. On fringe of business district, hence popular for visiting executives. Only a few blocks to Chinatown and Union Square. ****BEST BUY(1)

YORK HOTEL (100 rooms), 940 Sutter Leavenworth/Hyde), 885-6800 or 800-327-3608. This was a multi-million dollar renovation. Cabaret shows are held in the Plush Room--hotel guests are admitted at half price. *Rates include continental breakfast and limousine service to Fisherman's Wharf.* Single or double $84-$94, extra person $8. ****BEST BUY(1)

LA PETITE AUBERGE (28 rooms), 863 Bush (Mason/Taylor), 928-6000. *Rates include full breakfast and tea in the afternoon.* Decorated in antique French furnishings. Single-double $95-$125. ****BEST BUY(1)

INN AT THE OPERA (48 rooms), 333 Fulton (Franklin/Gough), 863-8400. This old hotel was restored in 1985 at cost of some $7 million. Was and still is the hotel for guest performers at the Opera. Some rooms are small. Single or double $95-$125, suites for 4 begin at $125. ****BEST BUY(10)

MILLFIORI INN (17 rooms), 444 Columbus (Vallejo), 433-9111. *Rates include continental breakfast.* Single $65, double $75, double-double, up to 4, $90. ****BEST BUY(3)

STEWART-GRINSELL HOUSE (5 rooms, 3 with bath), 2963 Laguna (Filbert), 563-3314. *Rates include continental breakfast.* Single without bath $50, double $70; single with bath $90, double with bath

$110. Handsomely restored Victorian residence, a few blocks from Union St. ****BEST BUY(6)

MARINA INN (40 rooms), 3110 Octavia (Lombard), 928-1000 or 800-338-4000. Renovated at cost of several million dollars in antiques, oriental rugs etc. *Rates include continental breakfast and free parking.* Rooms facing Lombard are noisy. Single $65, double $69. ****BEST BUY(6)

INN AT CASTRO (4 rooms), 321 Castro (17 St/Market), 861-0321. *Rates include continental breakfast.* Owner is interior decorator; he restored this Victorian in modern, luxurious decor. Single $80, double $85. ****BEST BUY(15)

EL DRISCO HOTEL (40 rooms), 2901 Pacific Ave. (Baker), 346-2880. Elegant, remodeled hotel in prestigious Pacific Heights, 20-30 minutes by bus to downtown S.F. Single $62, double $72, extra person $15; 2-room suite, up to 4 persons, $55-$120. ****BEST BUY(11)

Bed & Breakfast

The following is a list of hotels and inns that include breakfast in their room rates. Their full addresses and details are to be found in previous chapters of this book, under the appropriate headings, e.g., Economical. After this listing you will find the names & addresses of services that book private B&B accomodations.

Economical

Adelaide Inn
Obrero
Pension San Francisco
Grove Inn
Edward II
The Red Victoria
Diamond House
All Seasons
Shangri-La Inn

Intermediate

Beresford Arms
Oxford
UN Plaza
Cornell
Stanyan Park
Casa Arguello
Comfort Inn
Travelodge Civic Center
Pacific Heights Inn
Comfort Suites

Splurge

The Andrews
Millfiori
David
Redwood Inn
Vagabond Inn
Laurel Inn

Big Splurge

Cartwright
Diva
Kensington Park
Vintage Court
Juliana
York
Union Square
La Petite Auberge
Marina Inn
Inn at Castro

Referral Services

Bed & Breakfast (B&B) in private homes in San Francisco (as is common in England, for example) is relatively expensive, but for a reason. The hosts are carefully vetted, they supply a room with bath and breakfast and are located in good areas not too far from the city. In calculating the price, you must remember that breakfast is included and that *no tax is added*.

VISITOR'S ADVISORY SERVICE, 1506 Oak St., Alameda, CA 94801, 521-9366. B&B in San Francisco and Bay Area, Single $20 to $45, double $30-$65. The higher range is for rooms with private bath. This agency also offers furnished apartments for up to 4 persons for $350-$600 a week.

AMERICAN FAMILY INN, 2185A Union Street, San Francisco, 94123, 931-3083. This is a reservation service for bed-and-breakfast facilities in private homes in San Francisco, ranging from simple shared-bath to deluxe private-bath arrangement with hot tubs etc. Singles start at $35-$40 for shared-bath and $55 with private bath. Doubles are from $50 shared bath, $60-up private bath. Usually a minimum of 3 nights. At time of making the reservation, a one-night deposit is required.

ROOMSERVICE AND RESERVATIONS, 543-4522 (free call from out-of-state 800-325-6343). Reserves private B&B's from $30 (shared-bath) to $85, including breakfast. Also represents a number of the higher-priced inns, $55-$125 and more.

BED & BREAKFAST INFORMATION SERVICE, 641-0632. This is a service provided by the Inn San Francisco (see listing under Intermediate Hotels) at no charge. They will refer to some 15 other licensed Inns, not to private homes. But beware, some are very expensive.

Hotels with Kitchenettes or Kitchen Facilities

Hostels

San Francisco International
Marin Headlands
Point Reyes

Economical Hotels

European Guest House
Adelaide Inn
Gaylord

Chippendale
Gough-Hayes
Marina Motel
Jack's House
Hill Point Guest House
Ocean Park Motel

Intermediate Hotels

Beresford Arms
El Cortez
Mayflower Hotel Apartments

Splurge Hotels

Argyle
Laurel Motor Inn

Big Splurge Hotels

Executive Suites

V. Low-Priced Restaurants

Buffets

There are not many buffet restaurants in San Francisco and I believe they are worth listing for those who crave a buffet-style meal, either because it is very economical eating or because it is like being at a big party where there is a variety of fine food.

Buffets Up to $5

BEST BUY****

KUBLAI KHAN'S MONGOLIAN BBQ, 1160 POLK (Sutter), 885-1378. ll:30am-11pm, Fri-Sat to 1am. Lunch $4.50, dinner $6.95. On being seated you are served a Mongolian soup, an egg-roll, 2 pot-stickers and tea. You get up and choose from 4 sliced meats, various vegetables and diverse sauces which you then bring to a cook who prepares it on a stainless-steel stove, Korean-style. Return as often as you wish for more. Clean, attractive, tasty. **** BEST BUY(10)

MARCELLO'S PIZZA, corner Haight & Fillmore, 621-6700. All-you-can-eat pizza slices and salad bar, Mon & Tues only 5-8pm, $3.95, children under 10 $2.25. ****BEST BUY(14)

CAFE ORIENT (Chinese), 438 Castro (18/19 Sts), 863-6868. 12-2:30pm daily. $3.25. Up to 8 items, e.g., curry chicken, spareribs, egg rolls. ****BEST BUY(15)

VERY GOOD***

OLD EUROPE RESTAURANT, corner Larkin & Eddy, 449-8862. Buffet includes salad bar, $3.95. to 2:30pm. ***(9)

YOUNG'S (Chinese), 1731 Polk (Washington/ Clay), 775-4777. 11:30am-9:30pm. Lunch--$3.95, dinner $4.95. 10-12 items. No MSG. Also, large number of vegetarian & seafood dishes. ***(10)

CANTON RESTAURANT (Chinese), 524 Castro (18/19 Sts), 626-3604. 5-6 items $3.25, 11:30am-2:30pm Mon-Fri. ***(15)

GOLDEN PALACE (Chinese), 1830 Irving (19th Ave.), 566-5370. ll:30-2pm. Same as New Golden Palace. $3.15. ***(19)

NEW GOLDEN PALACE (Chinese), 250 West Portal Ave., 665-1193. 11:30am-2pm Mon-Fri, $3.49. Varies daily but usually consists of soup, chicken dish, beef dish, fried rice, fried noodles, tea. ***(21)

Buffets $5-$10

BEST BUY****

KUBLAI KHAN'S MONGOLIAN BBQ, 1160 Polk (Sutter), 885-1378. Dinner BBQ $6.75, Menu same as lunch. See Buffets Under $5 above for details. ****BEST BUY(10)

CHARLEY'S COUPE & CONSERVATORY, 2750 Leavenworth (Holiday Inn at Fisherman's Wharf), 776-8511. Price includes validated parking, glass of champagne. Lunch buffet $7.50, 11:30am-2:30pm, includes a hot fish entree, prawns, crab, seafood salads, and salad bar. Dinner buffet $13.95, 5:30-9:30 pm, consists of cold seafood items only, including oysters, smoked salmon, crab, seafood salads, salad bar, cheese, desserts. Sunday brunch buffet is only $11.95 and includes a hot entree plus the cold seafood evening items--an unusual value in an elegant restaurant setting. **** BEST BUY(4)

CHARLEY'S CAFE, Holiday Inn Annex, Beach and Leavenworth, Fisherman's Wharf, 771-9000. $6.95, Fri & Sat 5:30-10pm and Sun 11:30 am-4:30pm & 5:30-9pm. Price includes 1 glass of champagne. ****BEST BUY(4)

KURFUME (Japanese), 1375 9th Ave (Judah), 564-2127. 11am-10pm Mon-Fri, 5-10pm Sat-Sun. Hibachi BBQ $7.95. All-you-can-eat Sushi $8.95 Fri. ****BEST BUY(19)

VERY GOOD***

LOTUS, Holiday Inn, 750 Kearny (Washington/Clay), 433-6600, 11:30 am-2pm and 5-9pm Mon-Fri. $8.95. ***(8)

CAFE SANTE, 11 Clement (Arguello), 386-9792. Lunch $5.50. 1130am-5pm Mon-Sat. ***(22)

TOYO,(Japanese), 3226 Geary Blvd, 387-6564. All-you-can-eat Sushi $10. Small, simple, very clean. ***(13)

Buffets over $10

BEST BUY****

CARNELIAN ROOM, 52nd floor in Bank of America Bldg, 555 California (California/Montgomery), 433-7500. Sunday brunch, $17.50, children under 10 $9.75. 10am-2:30pm. Includes unlimited parking and champagne. Highest spot in town, spectacular. Big Splurge value. ****BEST BUY(8)

CATHEDRAL HILL HOTEL, 1101 Van Ness (Post), 776-8200. Sunday Brunch Concerts, featuring selected conservatory groups of talented young students, 11am-1pm. Includes the usual $15.95 buffet. The hotel will donate directly to the scholarship fund after each concert. A good combination, for a worthy cause. **** BEST BUY(10)

PALACE COURT, Sheraton-Palace Hotel, Market & New Montgomery, 392-8600. Sunday brunch, 10:30am-2pm. $21, children under 12 $12. Includes a Bloody Mary. Beautiful dining room, wonderful array of foods. Big Splurge value. ****BEST BUY(7)

VERY GOOD***

WHITE ELEPHANT, 490 Sutter (Powell, on 30th floor of Holiday Inn), 398-8900. Sunday brunch 10:30am-2:30pm. $14.95, includes complimentary champagne. ***(1)

FERRY PLAZA, 1 Ferry Plaza (behind Ferry Bldg), 391-8403. $15.95, includes complimentary champagne and validated parking. ***(8)

LEHR'S GREENHOUSE, 740 Sutter (Taylor), 474-6478. Sunday brunch. $11.95, includes Ramos gin fizz or other drink, a sumptuous buffet which features a number of cajun dishes. Garden setting. ***(1)

PAPAGAYOS, Holiday Inn Civic Center, 50 8th St. (Market), 626-6103. 11am-2pm & 5-9pm. $8.95. ***(7)

MIYAKO HOTEL, 1625 Post (Japan Center), 922-3200. Sunday brunch, $14.50 includes complimentary champagne, validated parking. ***(12)

KUI SHIN BO, Japan Center, E. Bldg, 922-9575. All-you-can-eat sushi $15. ***(12)

WELLINGTON'S, S.F. Marriot Hotel, 1250 Columbus (Fisherman's Wharf), 775-7555. 10am-2pm daily. $15.45, children under 12 $7.75. Price includes complimentary champagne, validated parking. ***(4)

Salad Bars, All You Can Eat

THE WHITE HORSE, 637 Sutter (Mason/Taylor, in Beresford Hotel), 771-1708. 11am-2pm. Salad bar alone is $4.25 but it is included in the price of the entree and that is a better deal. **** BEST BUY(1)

SIZZLER, Eddy & Leavenworth, in the Tenderloin, 775-1393. Salad bar at $4.79 (discount for seniors) is the best buy in the Bay Area. It includes avocado, various fruits, diverse salads and vegetables, cottage cheese, etc. This franchise is run by a non-profit organization which uses the profits for the benefit of the jobless in the Tenderloin, for drug-counselling and for aiding needy Seniors. For other Sizzler restaurants in the Bay Area (e.g., Colma, Daly City and San Rafael), see the phonebook. ****BEST BUY(7)

VILLA NOMA, 861 Geary (Larkin). 11am-10pm daily. $2.75, also included in full meal with steak and pasta $6.95. ****BEST BUY(1)

VICTORIA STATION, Embarcadero & Broadway, 433-4400. Salad bar includes soup at lunch 11:30am-2pm for $3.95 and dinnertime 5-10pm for $4.25. With an entree at lunch salad bar is $1.95 additional and at dinner it is included in the price of the entree. ****(BEST BUY)(8)

LEHR'S GREENHOUSE, 740 Sutter (Taylor), 474-6478. $6.95 at lunch 11:30am-3pm and $8.95 at dinner 5-10pm. Salad bar has some 60 items. ****BEST BUY(1)

KNIGHT'S, 363 Golden Gate (Larkin/Hyde), 861-3312. $3.25. 7am-4pm Mon-Fri. Some items change daily. ****BEST BUY(9)

BURGER KING, see phonebook for locations, 6am-9pm daily, 8am-6pm Sunday. Around $3. Salad bar has 18-20 items. 819 Van Ness Ave (Eddy) especially recommended. ****BEST BUY(10)

CARL'S JR., see phonebook for locations. Around $3. All locations recommended except Market St which I found unkempt on 2 occasions. ****BEST BUY

BULLSHEAD, 3745 Geary Blvd (Arguello/2Av), 668-2323 and 840 Ulloa (West Portal), 665-4350. Noon to 10pm except Sun 4-10pm. $3.50, with hamburger or sandwich $1.95 additional, included with steak entree. ****BEST BUY(13)

SIRLOIN & BREW UNLIMITED, 1040 Columbus (Chestnut/Francisco), 885-4910. $3.95, including all-you-can-drink sangria or soft drink. ****BEST BUY(3)

VERY GOOD***

ROUND TABLE PIZZA, see phonebook for locations. Around $2.50. ***

PASTEL'S, 1400 Market (Polk/ Fell), 626-7475, 7am-6pm, Sat 9am to 3pm. Sundays closed. $3.25, with soup $4.50. Cup of soup & salad $2.95. ***(7)

Cafeterias

The advantages of a cafeteria are: no tip is required, service is fast, and you can survey the field of offerings and walk out if you are not satisfied. Usually overlooked, except by those working there, are the cafeterias in the various hospitals and in some of the government buildings. There are also a number of large company cafeterias serving low-priced meals that are open to visitors. Anyone dressed properly can eat there. Some are: Bechtel Corporation, 50 Beale Street, 11-1:30pm; Crown Zellerbach, 1 Bush Street, 7:30am-3:30pm; Metropolitan Life, 425 Market Street, 6:30am-3:30pm; P.G.& E. 77 Beale Street, 6:30am-3:15pm. Shakle Corporation, 444 Market Street, 7am-3pm. They are very reasonable and serve good food.

BEST BUY****

BROTHER JUNIPER'S BREADBOX, 1065 Sutter (Larkin), 771-8929. 7am-7pm Mon-Fri, 7am-3pm Sat. 1/2 sandwich (large), soup of the day, green salad $2.50-$2.70. Club sandwich $2 half, $3.90 whole. Coffee with meal 10 cents, refill 5 cents. Also reasonable breakfasts. Atmosphere is very informal and friendly. The restaurant is run by the Raphael House, a dedicated charity group that provides shelter to needy families. ****BEST BUY(1)

LIPP'S, 201 9th St. (Howard), 552-3466. Mon-Sat 11am-3pm. Open for hamburgers, sandwiches and snacks to 6pm. Has comedy Nite Fridays (National Theater of the Deranged $5). 1/2-lb hamburger $3, with potato salad $4. The following, with potatoes and vegetable--hamburger steak $3.75, halibut steak $4.75, calamari steak $3.75, hot plates $4.50, knockwurst $3.50. Cup of soup and 1/2 sandwich $2.50, bowl clam chowder $1.50. Interesting atmosphere, good food. ****BEST BUY(7)

MANNING'S CAFETERIA, 1275 Market 2nd fl. Cup soup 91 cents, bowl $1.50; 1 egg 46 cents; baked lasagna or liver and onions, including vegetables & mashed potatoes, $2.85. ****BEST BUY(7)

PAPA JOE'S, 1412 Polk (Pine), 441-2115. 7am-4pm, Mon-Sat. Breakfast: 2 eggs, bacon, hash browns, toast $2.45; hot cakes $1.85, hamburger special (1/3 lb) with fries and salad $2.25. Deluxe hamburger with fries and salad $2.65. Joe's Special with fries or salad $3.25, chef salad $2.65. Tuna or chicken salad sandwich with soup and salad $2.25. ****BEST BUY(10)

THE GOLD POST, 2700 16th Street (Harrison), 552-4290. 6am-3:30pm, except Sat 7am-2pm. Charcoal broiled hamburger (1/2lb) with fries $2.75; country burger, fries, bacon egg and cheese $3.95; salads: mixed $1.95, avocado with shrimp $3.65, all with French bread, butter and dressing. Sandwiches from $1.95 (egg salad) to $3.60 (club). ****BEST BUY(16)

LA CUMBRE (Mexican), 515 Valencia (16th St), 863-8205. 11am-9pm daily. Tacos $1.35, burritos $1.80, super burrito $2, Mexican beer $1.35, 1/2 lb. rice or beans 85 cents. Most popular taco and burrito place in the Mission. ****BEST BUY(16)

TAQUERIA PANCHO VILLA (Mexican), 16th & Valencia Sts, 864-8840. 11am-10pm. Burritos (soft tortillas filled with meat, rice, beans)-- $2.65, Special (also cheese & guacamole) $3.35, Super (also sour cream) $3.90. Dinners--with rice, beans, salad, tortillas--roast pork $4.95, chicken $3.95, steak ranchero (with bell peppers, onions, tomatoes, mild salsa) $3.95, chile rellenos (Mexican pepper stuffed with Monterey Jack cheese & topped with tomato sauce) or tostado (open crisp tortilla with chicken, pork or beef & topped with lettuce, tomato & grated cheese) $3.95. Taco $1.55, flautas (tortillas stuffed with meat, guacamole & sour cream) $2.65. Garlic prawns $4.75, guacamole & chips $1.95. This Taqueria & El Toro (next listing), same owner, are giving La Cumbre stiff competition. Portions are huge and these very large Taquerias are always crowded. ****BEST BUY(16)

TAQUERIA EL TORO (Mexican), 17th & Valencia Sts, 431-3351. 11am-10pm. Same owners, same menu as Pancho Villas just above. ****BEST BUY(16)

LA OLLA (Mexican-Nicaraguan-Argentinian), 2417 Mission (20th St), 282-6086. 11:30am-9pm, Mon-Thurs, Fri and Sat to 10pm. Lunch--beef or tripe soup with bread or tortillas $2.75, crab soup $2.95, fried pork with plantains $3.25. Daily special with salad and rice $4.75. Dinner, charbroiled specialties, with salad, rice, French fries, tortilla or bread--Nicaraguan steak in strips $6.95; Argentinian steak (marinated), 12 oz, $8.95; loin pork $6.50; prawns in sauce $7.25. ****BEST BUY(16)

SIMPLE(*)--VERY GOOD(***)

Note: There are a number of cafeteria-style food stalls on Market Street, for several blocks between 5th & 9th Streets, which are worth checking out. The food is on display and often looks very attractive. The prices unusually low. You can eat lunch for as little as $2.

TAD'S, 120 Powell (Ellis), 982-1718. Served with baked potato, garlic roll and salad: steak $4.49, 1/2 broiled chicken $4.49, hamburger steak $3.79. Hamburger with cheese, salad and baked potato $2.49. ***(9)

FOOD CENTER (Chinese, Mexican, Philippine), 945 Market Street (5th/6th Sts), 543-3742. Simple. Consists of four food stalls and one large sitdown area. Combination plates $1.99-$2.40. Whole BBQ chicken $3.75, Chinese, Mexican & Philipine specials from 99 cents. Very simple but filling. ***(7)

SAM'S CHARCOAL HOFBRAU, 536 Golden Gate (Polk/Van Ness), 673-7633. One egg, toast, coffee $1.55; deluxe 1/2 lb. charbroiled hamburger with fries $3.30, N.Y., cut steak $4.65. ***(9)

DOUBLE-K RESTAURANT, 434 Larkin (Turk), 771-2739. 6:30am-6:30pm Mon-Fri 7:30am-6pm, Sat. Breakfast (6:30-11am): including potatoes, toast, coffee--sausage and 2 eggs $2.25, bacon and 1 egg $2. A la carte: 2 eggs $1, toast 40 cents. Daily specials include soup, dessert, coffee or tea--asparagus and chicken $3,50, roast pork $3. Many Chinese dishes, e.g. noodles with beef or pork $2.65, and up. (9)

HAPPI HOUSE TERIYAKI (Japanese), corner Van Ness and Sutter, 928-4728. Daily 11am-11pm. Fast food Japanese restaurant. Dishes with rice and chicken salad: beef pork or chicken teriyaki $3.45; mixed teriyaki $3.55, tempura (fish, shrimp, vegetable) $4.65; Pacific snapper $3.95, steak teriyaki $4.35. Udon noodle soup $1.50, cup rice 80 cents, cup chicken salad 90 cents, coffee (Kona) 50-60 cents, soft drinks 50-70 cents. ***(10)

THE BAGEL RESTAURANT (Jewish), corner Polk & Bush, 441-2212. 8am-9pm daily. Resembles a typical lower middle-class cafeteria in New York City, similar menu, e.g., Hungarian goulasch $4.95, brisket of beef $4.50, stuffed cabbage $4, bockwurst and beans or sauerkraut $3.20, borscht with sour cream $1 (bowl $1.75), 1/2 BBQ chicken $2.25, soup and sandwich $2.95. ***(10)

HAHN'S KOREAN BBQ, 1710 Polk (Clay), 776-1095. 11:30am-10pm except Sun. Fast-food Korean BBQ of good quality. With rice, salad, kimchee: beef or short ribs $3.50, pork spareribs $3.45, chicken $3.25, BBQ oysters $3.55, squid $3.50, shrimp $4.20, scallops $4.60. Udon (noodles) with beef $2.95, with pork $2.80, with shrimp $3.20, with vegetables $2.80; 6 potstickers $2.25. ***(10)

CHICKEN-N-COOP NO. 4, 3036 16 St. (Mission/Valencia), 982-1640. 8am-8pm. For other locations, see phone-book. 1/4 chicken, baked potato, salad, bread & butter $2.29. 2 whole BBQ chickens, 2 baked potatoes, 1 pint salad $8.99. 1/3-lb hamburger $2.19. Dinners--served with salad & potatoes--1/2 chicken $3.99, spareribs $4.99, roast beef or pastrami or ham $4.99. ***(16)

THE CHILI BOWL, 2599 Mission (22nd St) 282-1515. 9am-9pm daily. Chili and beans $1.35, ham and cheese sandwich $1.76, 1/4-lb. deluxe hamburger $2.02, soup or salad 65 cents, fish and chips $3. Prices include tax. **(16)

EL POLLO SUPREMO (Mexican), 3150 24th Street (Shotwell/South Van Ness), 550-1193. Whole chicken (8 pieces) $6.52, 1/2 chicken (4 pieces) $3.55, 1/4 chicken (2 pieces) $2.26, all served with tortillas and Mexican salsa. Corn on the cob 75 cents. Chicken is flattened and charbroiled, with Spanish sauce. ***(16)

TOKYO STOP (Japanese), 6050 Geary (25th Av) 387-8088, and 11th and Geary, 221 7867. 11-9pm daily. Take-out and eat-in, parking, Japanese fast food, e.g., sukyaki $2.85, tempura $2, udon (noodle soup) with vegetables, egg and crab $2.35, sashimi $2.90, salmon teriyaki $2.80. ***(15)

Hofbraus

These are the typical beer and carved-meat cafeterias, with adjoining bars. All are clean and have a distinctive atmosphere.

BEST BUY****

LEFTY O'DOUL'S, 333 Geary (Powell), 982-8900. 7am-11pm daily. Large sandwiches, large servings. Carved sandwiches $3.59. Regular dinner, including salad, potatoes & or vegetable--$6.30.

Daily special e.g., short ribs with potatoes and vegetables $4.39 (Tues and Fri), corned beef and cabbage (Thurs) $4.39, chicken (Sun) $4.95. Pies $1.25, coffee 40 cents, fresh fruit bowl $1.69. ****BEST BUY(1)

TOMMY'S JOYNT, corner Van Ness and Geary, 775-4216. 10am-2am daily. Very picturesque, very popular, beers from all over the world, large servings at the counter. Large carved sandwich on sour-dough roll $2.95, buffalo stew (specialty) $4.65, meat balls and spa-ghetti $3.65, meat plate with potatoes and vegetables $4.45, beer'n soup (specialty) 90 cents, large stein beer 85 cents, Heineken's $1. ****BEST BUY(10)

VERY GOOD***

MAIN STEM BRAUHAUS, corner Turk & Market, 776-3330. 10am-11pm. Hot sandwiches $2.95, Swiss cheese $1.99. Lunch spe-cials $3.50. Dinner plates, with side order, bread/butter, $4.99; turkey curry with rice $3.39; knockwurst with sauerkraut or beans $2.99, clam chowder or chili $1.59. Generous portions. ***(9)

HOFBRAU, 219 O'Farrell (Powell), 781-9068.7am-midnight. Hand-carved sandwiches $3.10--turkey, roast beef, corned beef, pastrami; hot sandwiches with mashed potatoes $3.90. Reuben, with 2 meats, $3.90. Lunch Special $4.50--sandwich, soup or salad, tea or coffee. German sausage with sauerkraut $3.75, dinner plates, with meat, salad, vegetables $5.80. ***(9)

Sandwiches

BEST BUY****

DEWEY'S, Powell & Geary (in St. Francis Hotel), 397-7000. 11am-3pm Mon-Fri, 11am-4pm Sat. Soup $3.50. Create-your-own sand-wich $5.50; soup & sandwich or salad $7; soup, salad and sandwich $7.75. Return as often as you wish. ****BEST BUY(1)

PARI'S DELI, 842 Geary St (Hyde/Larkin), 771-2219. This is a Mid-Eastern deli & grocery, also fresh meats & chicken. Super-sub, sev-eral meats & cheeses, $2.50; poor boy $2, crab sandwich $3.50, liverwurst $2, bagel dog $1.19. Piroshki $1.49, baklava 75 cents, cup noodle soup 80 cents. ****BEST BUY(1)

PAPA JOE'S, 1412 Polk (Pine), 441-2115. See under Cafeterias. ****BEST BUY(10).

THE SANDWICH PLACE.2029 Mission (16th-17th Sts), 431-3811. Lunch only, closed Sat-Sun. Foot-long Giant Sandwiches on French roll, e.g., hot pastrami with lettuce, tomato, peppers $3.25; Giant Combination with 4 meats and 2 cheeses $2.80; regular sandwiches $1.70-$2.90. Also "overstuffed" 24" party loaf $9. Bowl of chili $1.40, soup 70 cents. Probably the best sandwich value in all of the City and a favorite of mine. ****BEST BUY(16)

KIM'S MARKET, 1971 Fillmore (Pine), 771-9250. Ham and cheese on French roll 90 cents, others to $1.69. This is a deli meat market, good quality, incredible price. ****BEST BUY(11)

THE SNACK FACTORY, 2226 Polk (Green/Vallejo), 441-6730. Foot-long sub $4.25, 1/2 $2.25. Pastrami $2.50, roastbeef $2.65, hot dog 75 cents. ****BEST BUY(10)

SCANDINAVIAN DELICATESSEN & RESTAURANT, 2215 Market (Sanchez/Noe), 861-9903. Ham, pastrami, roast beef $1.70; bratwurst or salami $1.30, smoked salmon $2.95. ****BEST BUY(15)

LUCCA DELICATESSEN, 2120 Chestnut (Steiner), 921-7873. Lucca's special sandwich on 1 1/2 lb loaf of Italian bread with meat, cheese, olives, peppers, tomatoes, lettuce, mayonnaise and/or mustard, whole $11.50, half $5.80; 1/2 roast chicken and 1/2 pint of salad $3.30; whole chicken $4.15. ****BEST BUY(6)

ROSSI'S DELICATESSEN, 426 Castro (Market), 863-4533, 10am-7pm Mon-Sat. Specializes in Italian foods and sandwiches. A combination torpedo on French   roll, 10", $2.25; cheese cake 99 cents, falafel on pita bread $2.25, pizza slice (8"x10") $1.45. The combination torpedo is made in limited quantity each day, so order early. ****BEST BUY(15)

PURITY DELICATESSEN, 2069 24th St.(York), 282-6703. 10am-2:30pm Mon-Fri. Foot-long torpedo deluxe $3.99, soup $1.48-$1.69, BBQ hamburger $1.69. ***(16)

GOOD(**)-VERY GOOD(***)

BANH MI BALE, 611 Geary (Jones). Vietnamese hole-in-the-wall, cafeteria style. French submarine (ham, cheese, pate) $2; chef salad (ham, cheese, turkey, egg) $2.50; shrimp salad $3. Also Vietnamese dishes $4. **(1)

RANA'S SANDWICH SHOP, 440 Turk (Larkin), 928-2809. Lunch special: combination (4 meats and cheese), salad and drink $2.99; tuna salad $1.85; chicken salad $1.75; turkey sandwich $2.25; crab sandwich $2.39; crab salad 99 cents $3.49 (depending on size). ***(4)

BILL'S, 343 Kearny (Pine), 986-1052, 6am-4pm Mon-Fri. Financial district. Choice of some 20 sandwiches, 95 cents-$2.30, e.g., white meat turkey $1.95, ham and Swiss $1.75. ***(8)

SANDWICH ESTABLISHMENT, 652 Polk (Eddy), 776-9595, 9am-5pm. Combination sandwich consisting of 6 meats and 2 cheeses $3. Teriyaki beef sandwich $3. This restaurant also specializes in sushi, e.g., assorted sushi $3.10, other sushi $2-$5.95. ***(9)

J & E DELI, Larkin (O'Farrell), 673-2490, 5am-10pm daily. Combination sandwich (3 meats, 2 cheeses) on French roll $2.50; other sandwiches $1.75 (liverwurst)--$2.25 (pastrami), salads $1.35 a pint. Specialty: BBQ chicken 1/2 $1.99, whole $3.50. ***(9)

PETE'S DELI & CAFE, 1661 Divisadero (Sutter) 931-4800. 7am-7pm Mon-Fri. Greek and Mid-Eastern dishes and pastries. Sandwiches from $1.95 (liver sausage)-$2.55 (roast beef). Chef salad $2.55, Mid-Eastern plate $2.50. ***(11)

MR.SUBMARINE, 4 locations, see phone book. Their best deal is a foot-long submarine with 2 hams, Italian salami & cheese $3.35. Also, chili $1.25, soup $1.50. ***

RONA DELI, 1926 Lombard (Buchanan/Webster), 567-6206. Combination with 3 meats and 2 cheeses, $2.75. Bagel and creamcheese 95 cents. Whole BBQ chicken $4.95. ***(6)

BREAKFAST

Breakfast at many restaurants--especially in large hotels--can cost as much as lunch or dinner. But there are alternatives. Check the restaurants under Cafeterias in this book: most have breakfast specials. Also, it is worth checking restaurant and cafes in your area for specials. Here are some good choices:

THREE STAR BAKERY-DELI, 707 Sutter (Taylor), 885-0665. 7am-8pm daily. Breakfast (7-11am), bacon and eggs, toast, potatoes, coffee $1.99; juice and pancakes, coffee $1.49; orange juice, muffin, coffee $1.09. ***BEST BUY(1)

THE WHITE HORSE, 637 Sutter (Mason/Taylor), 771-1708. Breakfast 7:30-10:30am Mon-Fri. Continental breakfast with large juice, choice of muffin, toast or Danish, coffee $2.50. ****BEST BUY(1)

LITTLE HENRY'S, 995 Larkin (Geary/Post) 776-1757. 11am-10pm daily except Sun. With potatoes, toast, butter--2 eggs, ham, sausage or bacon $2.50; 2 eggs, toast $1.75; hot cakes or French toast $1.85; Joe's Special (ground beef, spinach, eggs) $2.95. ****BEST BUY(1)

LUCKY CAFE, 655 Larkin (Ellis), 673-5207. 1 egg, toast, hash brown, sausage $1.99. 1 egg, 2 hot cakes, 2 bacon or sausage $1.99. ****BEST BUY(9)

MOULIN ROUGE, 807 Geary (Larkin), 928-0158. Cafeteria. 2 eggs, toast, bowl fruit, coffee, $2.39; 2 hot cakes, 1 egg, bowl fruit, coffee, $2.39; 2 eggs, ham, bacon or sausage $1.99. Omelettes (3 eggs) with hash browns, butter, jelly $2.60 (plain) or $2.90 (cheese). ***(1)

AUNT MARY'S (Mexican-Salvadoran), 3122 16th Street (Valencia), 626-5523. Specials, only 7-10am: 2 pancakes, 2 strips bacon, 1 egg $1.49; 2 eggs, hash browns, toast, jelly $1.49; huevos rancheros with Jack cheese, rice, beans, tortilla, coffee $2.95. ****BEST BUY(16)

GOOD(*) TO VERY GOOD(***)

HANKEN'S COFFEE SHOP, 601 Sutter (Mason), 885-4014. 7am-9pm Mon-Fri, 7am-3pm Sat & Sun. Continental breakfast with muffin, toast or Danish $2.50. **(1)

VALLEY CAFE, 1089 Sutter (Larkin), 885-4412. 8am-7:30pm daily. 2 eggs, toast, hash browns $1.75, 3 eggs $2.25. Toast, butter, jelly 50 cents, raisin toast 65 cents. 1 egg 65 cents, 2 eggs $1.10, hot oatmeal 90 cents, tea or coffee 45 cents. ***(1)

FOOD WORKS RESTAURANT, 491 Pine (Kearny), 398-2342. 6am-4pm Mon-Fri. 2 eggs, toast, coffee $1.35, with bacon $1.90. ***(8)

TINA'S RESTAURANT, 83 Eddy (Mason), 982-3451. 6am-6pm daily. Breakfast (to 11am): 2 hot cakes, 2 bacon strips, 1 egg, juice $2.65; 2 hot cakes, 2 sausages, 2 eggs, coffee $2.95. ***(9)

TAD'S, 120 POWELL (Ellis), 982-1718. Breakfast, 7am-noon. Cafeteria. 2 eggs, potatoes, toast $2.29; 2 hot cakes, 2 eggs $2.29; breakfast cereal $1. **(9)

JIM'S COUNTRY KITCHEN, 235 Church (Market), 621-3040. 6:30am-9:30 pm. Country breakfast: ham, bacon or sausage, 2 eggs any style, 2 hot cakes, $3.15; continental breakfast $1.50. ***(15)

CHURCH STREET STATION, Corner Church & Market, 861-1266. Open 24 hours, daily. Breakfast special: ranch eggs, potatoes, toast, jelly $2.35, coffee 52 cents; omelette, fries, toast, jelly $2.90. Danish $1.10, cold plate $3.95. Well drinks 99 cents. ***(15)

UPTON, 2419 Lombard (Scott), 567-1335. 2 eggs with bacon & sausage or ham & 4 pancakes $1.99. ***(6)

SUM'S, 2450 Noriega (31/32 Avs), 665-6603. 2 eggs, potatoes, toast $1.40. ***(20)

Lunch up to $5

Chinese lunches

A large number of first-class Chinese restaurants offer special lunches, from 11am-3pm (some to 2:30 only) at prices ranging from $2.25-$3.95. Most are for weekdays only, not holidays, but a few include weekends as well. The lunch usually consists of soup, tea, a main dish over rice and tea. Often there is a choice of 10 or more entrees; others keep the list short. Listed below are a number of such restaurants. Most are also suited for evening and weekend dining. Be sure to ask for the special lunch menu since the restaurants often give tourists the regular menu first.

BEST BUY****

LOTUS GARDEN, 632 Grant (Pine), 397-0130. 11:30-2:30pm. $3.45-$3.95. See also under Vegetarian. ****BEST BUY(2)

CHUNG KING, (Szechuan), 606 Jackson (Kearny/Grant), 963-3899. $2.95-$3.25. A favorite. ****BEST BUY(2)

JADE GARDEN, 674 Broadway (Stockton/Grant), 956-4027. $3-$3.50. 58 items on menu. 11am-4:30pm. ****BEST BUY(2)

SZECHUAN, 2209 Polk (Green/Vallejo), 474-8282. $3.30. ****BEST BUY(10)

TAI CHI, 2031 Polk (Broadway/Vallejo), 441-6758. $3.25. A favorite; I especially like the sweet-sour shrimp and tomatobeef. ****BEST BUY(10)

SZECHUAN TASTE, 1545 Polk (Pine), 928-1379. $3.25-$3.79. ****BEST BUY(12)

SAN WONG, 1682 Post (Buchanan/Japantown), 921-1453. $3.25. ****BEST BUY(12)

SZECHUAN VILLAGE, 3317 Steiner (Lombard/Chestnut), 567-9989. $3.25-$4.25. ****BEST BUY(6)

RED CRANE, 1115 Clement (12 Av), 751-7226. $2.85. A favorite. **** BEST BUY(22)

TSING TAO, 3107 Clement (32 Av), 387-2344. $2.75-$3.75. A longtime favorite, worth the trip. ****BEST BUY(23)

HARBIN, 327   Balbao (4/5 Avs) 387-0247. $3.95. ****BEST BUY(19)

CHINA HOUSE, Balbao (6 Av), 386-8858. $2.80-$3.25. ****BEST BUY(19)

VERY GOOD***

OLD PEKING, 655 Jackson (Kearny/ Grant), 391-2996. $2.85. ***(2)

HUNA HOMES, 622 Jackson (Kearny), 982-2844. $3.25-$3.95. ***(2)

SZECHUAN GRAND, 614 Jackson (Kearny/Grant), 397-1650. $2.50-$3.25. ***(2)

TAO TAO, 675 Jackson (Grant), 982-6125. $3.25. ***(2)

YU SU YUAN, 638 Pacific (Kearny/Grant), 986-7386. $3.15. ***(2)

FORTUNE, 675 Broadway (Stockton/Grant), 421-8130. $2.95. ***(2)

OCEAN KING SEAFOOD RESTAURANT, 684 Broadway (Stockton), 989-8821. $2.75-$5.25. ***(2)

SUNYA, 823 Clay (Grant/Stockton), 362-9612. $2.5o-$4. ***(2)

CHINA INN, 1331 Polk (Pine), 885-1896. $3.50-$3.95. ***(10)

HUNAN ON POLK, 1150 Polk (Sutter), 771-6888. $2.75. ***(10)

CHEF YEE, 1695 Polk (Clay), 771-8989. $3.50-$4.50. ***(10)

IMPERIAL CHINA, 2401 Polk (Union), 776-7303. 11:30am-4pm. $3.75. 3 choices: sweet-sour pork, curry chicken, beef & vegetables. ***(10)

FIRST HUNAN, 1828 Divisadero (Pine/Bush), 346-8235. $2.95. ***(11)

HAPPY FAMILY, 3727 Geary (Arguello), 221-5095. $2.95-$3.50. ***(13)

NEW WORLD, 736 Clement (8/9 Avs), 221-1410. $2.75. ***(22)

CHAN'S CHINESE KITCHEN, 336 Clement (4 Av), 387-8370. $2.65. ***(22)

FOUNTAIN COURT, (Shanghai style), 354 Clement (5 Av), 668-1100. $2.99. ***(22)

HYATT GARDEN, 908 Clement (10 Av), 221-0224. $2.85. ***(22)

GOLDEN CITY, 2253 Irving (24 Av), 661-1226. $2.95-$3.50. Includes fried chicken or egg roll. Also on Sat. Choice of 27 entrees, 8 spicy. ***(20)

HA'S (Chinese), 2333 Irving (24/25 Avs), 665-6033. Also on Sat and Sun. $2.95 & $3.25 (prawns or shrimp). Choice of 21 entrees, 11 spicy. ***(20)

DRAGON HOUSE, 5344 Geary Blvd (18 Av), 751-6545. $2.80. Choice of 15 dishes. ***(13)

BIN KIANG, 3420 Balboa (35/36 Avs), 752-4009. $3.95. ***(20)

Other low-priced ethnic lunches

BEST BUY****

INDONESIA RESTAURANT, 678 Post (Jones), 474-4026. $2.75. ****BEST BUY(1)

AZUMA (Japanese), 3520 20th St. (Mission/Valencia), 282-1952. $3-$3.50. ****BEST BUY(16)

CHERRY FLOWER (Vietnamese), 124 Columbus (Broadway), 398-9101. $3.50. ****BEST BUY(2)

MEKONG, (Vietnamese), 930 Larkin (Ellis), 928-8989. $3.75. ****BEST BUY(9)

KOREAN PALACE, 631 O'Farrell (Leavenworth), 771-5353. $4.75-$5.95. ****BEST BUY(9)

VERY GOOD***

MAY SUN (Japanese/Chinese), 1748 Fillmore (Sutter), 567-7789. $3.25-$3.75. ***(11)

LA PIRAMIDE (Mexican), 1707 Haight (Cole), 221-0719. $3. ***(13)

HANIM'S GRILL (Indonesian), 138 Church (Market), 621-8390. $3.95. ***(15)

MOMO (Japanese), 3232 Scott (Chestnut/Lombard), Mon-Fri except Wed. $4.25. ***(6)

CELIA'S (Mexican), 2424 Lombard (Scott), 922-8437 & 4019 Judah (45/46 Avs), 564-0662. $3.25. ***(6)(13)

HANIL KWAN (Korean), 1802 Balboa (19 Av), 732-4447. $4.50. ***(13)

TOMMY'S (Mexican), 5929 Geary Blvd (23/24 Avs), 387-4747. 11am-4pm. $3.60. ***(13)

SAIGON MOI (Vietnamese), 4128 Geary (6 Av), 221-7895. $2.95. ***(13)

TOYO RESTAURANT, (Japanese), 3226 Geary (Spruce/Parker), 387-6564. $2.95. ***(13)

SHENSON'S Deli (Jewish), 5120 Geary Blvd (15/16 Avs), 751-4699. $4.50. ***(13)

TAKEYA (Japanese), 5850 Geary Blvd (22/23 Avs), 386-2777. 11am-9:30pm, 5-9:30pm Sat, closed Sun. Mon-Fri, $4.10-$5.50, includes soup, rice, pickle, green tea and entree. ***(13)

SKYDRAGON (Vietnamese), 914 Clement (10/11 Avs), 752-7480. $3,25. ***(22)

HAHN'S HIBACHI (Korean), 2121 Clement (22/23 Avs), 221-4246. $3.95-$4.25. ***(23)

RAMA THAI, 3242 Scott (Lombard/Chestnut), 922-1599. $2.95-$3.25, including salad and tea. ***(6)

Chinese-American lunches and dinners

Chinese-American is a good sign to look for if you want a full-course meal for under $5. The meal usually consists of soup or salad, entree with potatoes and vegetable, dessert and coffee or tea, for--believe it or not!-- $2.50-$4.95, a dollar or two more if you order prime rib or steak. The restaurants are often cafeterias, with plain tables, some even a bit rundown or seedy-looking but very often serving good, wholesome food. If the place is new to you, check the decor, take a good look at the diners--more often than not seniors with low income or local Chinese--and make your decision. The prices shown below are for a complete meal.

JING KEUNG (Chinese), 655 Jackson (Grant/ Kearny), 391-2996. 7:30am-10:30pm. American menu changes daily. Here is a Friday menu: clam chowder, entree and jello or ice cream, e.g., fried filet sole & tartar sauce $2.95, fried scallops, pork chops or veal cutlet $3.50, half chicken $3.35. Also extensive Chinese menu of noodle and rice dishes in the $2.25-$3.95 range. ***(2)

EASTERN BAKERY & RESTAURANT (Chinese), 720 Grant (Sacramento), 392-4927. 8am-7pm daily. Entrees, with soup & dessert, $3.15-$3.55. ***(2)

UNCLE'S CAFE (Chinese), 65 Waverly Place (corner of Clay between Grant & Stockton), 982-1954. $3.75-$4.10, e.g., spareribs, lamb curry, pot roast with soup & dessert. Also, full Chinese menu at low prices. Very popular with Chinese. ****BEST BUY(2)

NEW JACKSON CAFE, 640 Jackson (Grant), 986-9717. 11am-9:30pm daily. Entrees, with soup & dessert, e.g., roast pork loin $3.75, beef tongue $3.75, calves liver/onions $3.75, prime rib $5.75. ****BEST BUY(2)

PING YUEN BAKERY, 650 Jackson (Grant), 986-6830. 7am-7pm daily. Entrees, with soup & dessert, e.g., calves liver $4, veal, wienerschnitzel or lamb curry $4.30, prime rib $5.95. Recently, a prominent restaurant critic praised the cuisine as being close to gourmet. ****BEST BUY(2)

VALLEY CAFE, 1089 Sutter (Larkin), 885-4412. Entrees, with soup & dessert, $3.50-$4.95. ****BEST BUY(1)

GOLDEN GATE COFFEE SHOP, 937 Geary (Larkin/Polk), 771-1877. 11am-10pm. Entrees, with soup & dessert, $3.15-$3.95, e.g., Korean BBQ $3.55, beef teriyaki $3.45, lamb chops $3.55. ****BEST BUY(1)

LUCKY CAFE, 655 Larkin (Ellis), 673-5207. 8am-6pm except Mon. Entrees, with soup or salad & dessert--pork chops $4, breaded veal cutlet $3.25, liver/onions $3.10, filet sole $3.50. Coffee or tea 40 cents, soft drinks 60 cents. ***(9)

HAPPY BEAR, 655 Ellis (in Travelodge), 771-3000. 7am-9pm. Including soup or salad--grilled salmon $4.95, liver/onions $3.50, fried chicken $3.95, steak $4.95. ***(9)

J & K RESTAURANT, 1125 Market (7/8 Sts), 552-5066. Lunch & dinner specials with soup, coffee or tea and dessert $3.95, e.g., baked chicken, calves liver with bacon & onion. ***(7)

SUPERIOR RESTAURANT, 312 8th Ave. (Clement), 221-9165. 8am-3:30pm except Sun. 1/2-lb hamburger with fries $3.60, chef salad $3.25, chicken-in-a-basket and fries $3.55, scallops and vegetables, potatoes $3.95, fish and chips with salad $3.15, veal cutlet, vegetables, potatoes and bread $3.15. ***(22)

Other Low-Priced Restaurants Under $5

SALMAGUNDI (Continental), 442 Geary (Taylor) 441-0894. Cafeteria-style.11am-midnight. See other locations in phone book. Their specialty is soup and quiche. Soup of the day $2.75 and you can return once for a refill. Soup of the day with beverage and salad $4.65 (no seconds on soup); soup & fruit salad $4.10, quiche & salad $4.25, French roll and butter 65 cents, breakfast quiche $1.50, with French roll & butter $1.95. ***(1)

LITTLE OMAR'S (Armenian), 208 Powell (Taylor), 781-1010. 8am-6pm. For an interesting quick lunch--piroshki & salad $5, quiche Lorraine & salad $4.75, meza a la Omar (mixed Armenian appetizers) $5, yogourt soup with meatballs $2.25, yogourt with rose-petal preserves 75 cents. ****BEST BUY(9)

MAX FRIED CHICKEN (Filipino), 424 Geary (Taylor/Mason), 928-1987. 1/2 chicken $3.20, whole $6.40; fried chicken dinner, including soup or salad, coffee or soft drink, $5.50; chicken-steak combination with French fries $6.50. Interesting Philippine dishes $3-$6.95, desserts $1-$2.50. ****BEST BUY(1)

RAINBOW GARDEN (Vietnamese), 101 Eddy (Mason), 776-7122. llam-9:30pm except Sun. A number of dishes over rice $2.95-$3.25 e.g.,BBQ pork, squid, beef with mushrooms, chicken with mint leaves. Shrimp and pork salad rolls $3.25, noodle soup with pork, squid, sausage & fish cake $3.25; fried whole fish $4.95, beef dishes in firepot $4.95-6.50. At edge of Tenderloin but okay during day. A favorite. ****BEST BUY(9)

INDONESIA RESTAURANT, 678 Post (Jones), 474-4026. 10am-llpm. Simple, small restaurant (8 tables) with charm, good food and low prices. All dishes with rice, e.g., chicken curry $2.85, coconut beef $2.95, shrimp and egg $3.25, combination (interesting for introduction to Indonesian food) $3.15. Indonesian vegetable soup (spicy) 80 cents. Mixed salad with peanut sauce $1.75. Satay $2.50. ****BEST BUY(1)

TU LAN (Vietnamese), 8 Sixth St (Market/Mission), 626-0927. Looks sleazy, 1 row of tables & counter, but great food. Seafood dinner for 2, soup & 3 dishes, $8.15 per person. Beef or chicken noodle soup $3.50, various noodle, chicken, beef or pork dishes $3.25-4.50. Family dinner, including sour chicken soup, combination salad, pork shish-kebab, imperial roll, rice, cookie, tea $7.50 per person. aBreakfast $1.75 2 eggs, hash browns, toast, jam; with ham $2.25. ****BEST BUY(7)

BECK'S KOFFEE KORNER, (Sutter & Leavenworth), 885-5889. 7:30am-3pm. Daily Special, e.g., breaded veal cutlet with spaghetti $3.05, crabmeat omelette with soup & coffee $3.85. Waffles or pancakes with whipped butter & maple syrup $1.75. ***(1)

LITTLE HENRY'S (Italian), 995 Larkin (Geary/Post), 474-5276. 7am-9pm Tues-Sun. Joe's Special (ground beef & spinach) $2.95, N.Y. steak with soup or salad $5.95, spaghetti with mushrooms $3.75, fettucini al-pesto $3.95. ****BEST BUY(1)

ANH THUR (Vietnamese), 442 Hyde (O'Farrell), 885-5632. 6am-6pm, closed Sun. French submarine sandwich $1.50, French bread with sauced meatballs $1.50. Rice noodles--with meatballs $3, with imperial roll $2.80, combination seafood $3. Rice--with pork chop or beef stew $3; rice cake with Vietnamese ham $2.25. Coffee 30-60 cents, dessert $1, imperial roll 60 cents. Simple, hole-in-the-wall. ****BEST BUY(9)

RASA SAYANG (Malaysian, Singapore cuisine), 854 Washington (Grant/Stockton), 362-8239. Rice--with lamb, beef or curry chicken, cucumber & tomato $3.50. Noodles--with pork or beef, shrimp, egg $3.50; with round noodles, pork, shrimp, squid $3.75; with fish curry & prawns $3.50. Satay--beef or chicken on skewers, peanut sauce $4.50. Steamed fish $6, chicken curry $4.50, spring rolls $2.50, fried chicken $2.50. As far as I know, first Malaysian restaurant in the City, a good addition. ****BEST BUY(2)

GOLDEN DRAGON (Chinese), 883 Washington (Grant/Stockton), 398-3920. 8am-11pm daily. Don't confuse this bustling restaurant and take-out place with the large restaurant of the same name across the street, which has the same ownership but is more expensive. Wonton soup with noodles $2.10, braised noodles with beef stew $3.25, beef and rice $2.55, spare ribs with rice $2.55, shrimp and rice $3.70, beef chow mein $3.25. Large choice of rice-porridge dishes. ****BEST BUY(2)

HON'S WON TON HOUSE, 648 Kearny (Clay), 433-3966. This restaurant serves won ton in various forms and a few dishes over rice or noodles (made on premises). Noodle soup $1.70, won ton & noodle soup $2.10, brisket of beef & noodle soup $2.25, shrimp dumpling soup $2.45. BBQ pork over rice $2.80, curry beef over rice $3.50. Tea is included. ****BEST BUY(8)

SAM WOH (Chinese), 813 Washington (Grant/Stockton), 982-0596. 11am-3am, closed Sun. Probably most famous bare-bones restaurant in Chinatown. You walk alongside kitchen up narrow stairs to 2 more levels. Food is good, cheap. Stick to simple dishes like won ton soup with pork or chicken (enough for 4 as first course) $2.40, chicken with greens $3.30, roast pork with noodles $2.80, chow fun (fried rice noodles) with greens and chicken $2.90, prawns with greens and rice $3.20, porridge (thick rice soup) $2.15-2.50. ****BEST BUY(2)

GREAT WALL (Chinese), 815 Washington (next to Sam Woh), 397-5826. 11am-10pm Wed-Mon. Chicken with onions $4, assorted meats & bean curd $3.65, bean cakes with meat & vegetables $3.85. Rice soups $1.70-$2.40. Also, large variety of soups, pork, beef, chicken and fish dishes in the $3-$5 range. ****BEST BUY(2)

FRANTHAI (Chinese, Thai), 939 Kearny (Pacific), 397 -3543, 11:30am-10pm. Thai & Hunan cuisine. Thai & Hunan cuisine. Vegetarian Thai salad $3.95, hot-sour soup $3.95, Hunan eggplant $4.95, seafood chow mein $4.50, Thai noodles with shrimp, chicken, peanuts $4.95. Praised by critics as one of the best low-priced restaurants in the area. ****BEST BUY(2)

OCEAN SKY (Chinese), 641 Jackson (Grant/Kearny), 433-6802. Lunch 11am-3pm. Curry beef over rice $2.50, spareribs over rice $2.50, beef chow mein $2.50, noodles or won ton in broth $1.75-$2.50, porridge dishes $1.75-$2.50, ****BEST BUY(2)

WAH DO (Chinese), 615 Jackson, 362-2800. 11:30am-10pm. Hot-sour soup $2.40, almond chicken $4.75, prawns with green peas $5.95, pork with hot sauce $4.50 Chinese vegetables $3. ****BEST BUY(2)

HOTEL CARLTON (American), 1075 Sutter (Larkin), 673-0242. 7am-2pm & 5-9pm. Lunch, including soup and vegetables, potatoes or rice--fried chicken $4.95, calves liver $3.95, filet sole almadine $4.50, chocolate sundae $1, deluxe hamburger $2.95. ****BEST BUY(1)

MEKONG (Vietnamese), 730 Larkin (Ellis/O'Farrell), 928-8989. 9am-9pm. Crab meat with corn soup $2.95, lemon-grass BBQ spareribs $4.25, BBQ beef $4.25, coconut chicken $3.95. ****BEST BUY(7)

HONG KONG (Chinese), 245 Church (Market), 621-3020. 11:30am-9:30 pm, closed Sun. BBQ pork with noodle soup or won ton $2.20, shrimp or beef curry $3.50, pork with mixed vegetables $2.75, almond chicken or ginger beef $2.95, hot spiced beef $3.95, mixed vegetables $2.50, pepper beef or chicken $3.25. ****BEST BUY(15)

314 CHURCH (Japanese) (15 St), no name, no phone but jammed each lunch & dinner, so come early. 6 pieces sashimi with rice $3.60, 9 pieces $4.90, 6 pieces octopus $3.60. Cooked fish or sushi with rice--eel $4.95, shrimp $3.30, salmon $3.65. Spinach or avocado with soy sauce 90 cents. A find. ****BEST BUY(15)

SCANDINAVIAN DELICATESSEN & RESTAURANT, 2215 Market (Sanchez and Noe), 861-9913. 8am-8:30pm Mon-Fri. Cafeteria-style. Lunches and dinners with vegetables, potatoes, and choice of salad, bread and butter--Danish stew $2.75, Polish sausage $3.50, Swedish meat balls $3.50, veal curry $3.25, stuffed cabbage $3.25, cold plate $4.50, pork roast $4.50, Norwegian beef soups $1.75. Beers, soft drinks at deli prices. No nonsense, self-service, very large portions of wholesome food at a low price. ****BEST BUY(15)

NEW CENTRAL (Mexican, Peruvian), 301 S. Van Ness (14 St), 431-8587. 8am-8:30pm, to 6pm Sun. *Note*: The printed menu describes the dishes in English. Nachos $2.50, guacamole with chips $2.75, quesadilla $2, tortillas $1.75. Lunch--served with refried beans, Spanish rice, homemade tortillas & butter--flauta $3.75, tostada $3.75, burrito $3.75, enchilada $3.75, chile relleno $3.75, Taco $3.75, steak ranchero $4.75, carnitas $4.75. Dinner--served with beans, Spanish rice, salad, tortillas, chips & butter--same items as lunch only $0.75-$1 more for larger portions plus salad. Also for dinner--combination dish (create your own, 2 items) $5, beef rib steak $6, 1/2 deep-fried chicken $6. Birria (lamb stew) and menudo (tripe) served on Sat-Sun $4. Businessman's lunch, 11am-2pm Mon-Fri $3.25, one dish--flauta, taco, chile relleno, enchilada, tostada, taco de carne asada, or burrito. Burritos to go, made with rice & beans $2.50-$3. I consider this restaurant and Chava (see next listing) the 2 best family-type restaurants in the Mission. If hard-pressed, I'd give Chava a slight advantage but both serve wonderful food cheaply, and healthy portions. ****BEST BUY(16)

CHAVA (Mexican), 18th & Shotwell, 552-9387. (also CHAVA No. 2 at 570 4th St. which I have not been to). 11am-6pm. Machaca $5, huevos rancheros or Mexicana $4.50, birria (lamb stew) $4, tacos carne asada $2.75, burritos carne asada $3, quesadillos $2.25, chile rellenos $4.50, tripe soup (menudo grande) $5, galena mole (chicken with chocolate mole sauce) $4.50, tortas de camarones $4.50. Some experts say "best tortillas in town"; when you see the local crowd that fills the place, there seems no doubt. I especially liked the taco carne asada and camerones rancheros. ****BEST BUY(16)

AZUMA (Japanese), 3520 20th St. (Mission/Valencia), 2821952. 11am-2:30pm, 5-10pm, closed Sunday. Fried noodles or rice with beef and vegetables $3.50, shrimp with cucumbers $3.50, fish or beef teriyaki $5.50. ****BEST BUY(16)

EL TAZUMAL (Salvadoran), 3522 20th St (Valencia/Mission), 550-0935. 10am-10pm daily. Soups, tripe, bean or chicken $3.50. Lunch entrees from $3.95, e.g., liver and onions, pork chops, beef tongue in sauce. See also under Intermediate Restaurants. ****BEST BUY(16)

LA VICTORIA (Mexican), 2937 24th St.(Alabama), 550-9309. 10:30am-l0pm daily. Two tacos, rice and beans $4.05; 2 tostados, rice and beans $4.80; Machaca (meat, onion, chili, eggs, sausage) $5.70; steak ranchero, rice and beans $5.50; combination (chili rellenos, tamales, taco, rice and beans) $5.50. Birria (lamb or goat stew) $5.50. This is a family-run restaurant in simple surroundings. A favorite. ****BEST BUY(16)

ROYAL KITCHEN (Chinese), 3253 Mission (29 St), 824-4219. 11am-9pm, Sunday 2-9pm, closed Tues. Sweet-sour pork $3.95, sizzling fried prawns $5.75, chicken almond $4.25, mixed vegetables $3.50, pot stickers $3.25. ****BEST BUY(16)

HANA (Japanese), 408 Irving (5th & 6th Avs, near UC Hospital), 665-3952. 11:30am-2pm. Mon-Fri lunch, 5-9pm dinner Mon-Sat. Very popular; if you want a seat at lunch, be sure to get there before noon. Lunch includes soup, pickled cabbage, tea and casseroles over rice--beef, vegetables $3.70, teriyaki (barbecued beef $3.70, tempura (vegetables & shrimp) $3.70. Beef bowl $3.25, chicken teriyaki $3.50, noodles in broth with shrimp and vegetables $3.70. A favorite. **** BEST BUY(19)

OUR FATHER'S HOUSE, 1410 Clement (13 Av), 751-2429. 11:30am-7pm except Sunday. This is a bookstore cafe run by Jewish Christians. Interesting atmosphere and good food. Soups $1.25 cup, $2.25 bowl; bowl soup with home salad, bread & butter $4.75; quiche $2.75; quiche with bowl soup or home salad $4.75; pate, cup soup, bread & butter $4.95. ****BEST BUY(22)

VICTORIA (Vietnamese), 4128 Geary Blvd (5-6 Avs), 751-6697. 11:30 am-10pm, closed Mon. Crab meat & asparagus soup $2.75, lemon grass chicken $4.75, spicy fish in clay pot $4.95, BBQ pork in garlic sauce & lemon grass $4.95, spicy prawns $5.95, banana flambe $1.25. ****BEST BUY(13)

PHILIPPINE, 3619 Balboa (37 Av), 752-8657. Wed-Sun 11am-10pm, Sun to 8pm. Dinner includes soup or lumpia & rice--chicken adobo $3.99, beef & snow peas $3.99, beef asado $4.50, stewed pork & eggplant $4.99, adobo squid $5.99. ****BEST BUY(20)

EAGLE HOT SPOT (American & Philippine), 1240 Noriega (19 Ave), 661-5593. BBQ with baked beans, roll or rice and salad bar--pork or beef ribs $4.95, chicken or pork adobo $3.95. Salad bar (5 items) $2, with sandwich $1 extra. BBQ brisket and fries $3.75, steak $4.95. With potatoes, vegetables, salad bar & dessert--T-bone steak $7.95, countryfried chicken $4.95. ****BEST BUY(20)

VERY GOOD***

SILVER RESTAURANT (Chinese), 737 Washington (Grant/Kearny), 433-8888. *Open 24 hours*. Specialize in rice and noodle combinations. Porridge dishes $2.10-$2.85, noodles in soup $1.85-$3.20, chow mein & chow fun (noodles) $3.25-$4.05, BBQ items $3.25-$4.50. ***(2)

SUN YA (Chinese), 823 Clay (Grant/Stockton), 362-9612. 11:30-9pm. Hotsour soup $3.25, won-ton soup $1.95, prawns & snow peas $4.75, beef & tender greens $3.25, tomato or curry beef $3.25, almond chicken $3.75, pineapple chicken $4. ***(2)

A-1 CAFE (Chinese), 779 Clay (Grant/Stockton), 421-1666. 7am-3am. Porridge dishes $2.25-3.25; noodles in soup with meat or fish $2.25-$3; chow mein with chicken or meat $2.50-$3; rice plates with chicken, fish or meat $2.50-$3; Rice in bowl with chicken or meat, served only 11am-3pm, $2.50-$2.75. ***(2)

OCEAN GARDEN (Chinese), 735 Jackson (Grant/Stockton), 421-9129. 11:30am-12am. Hot-sour soup $3.75, szechuan beef $4.75, mushi pork $4.75, rock cod with pork & garlic (clay pot) $4.50, beef with ginger & pineapple (clay pot) $4.50 ***(2)

CORDON BLEU (Vietnamese), 771 O'Farrell (Larkin & Hyde), 441-4581, or 1574 California (Polk), 673-5637, 11am-10pm Tues-Sun. Special luncheons are $2.70-$3.90, e.g., 2 imperial rolls, chicken salad, meat sauce over rice $2.75. ***(9) (10)

THAI-BINH-DUONG (Vietnamese), 601 Larkin (Eddy), 673-7604. 8am-5pm. 7 tables, simple, clean. Large bowl Vietnamese beef noodle soup, 12 varieties, $2.95, with meat balls $3.50. Vietnamese rice noodles with pork, beef, or spring rolls $2.95-$3.50. Ice tea 35 cents. ***(9)

RACHA (Thai), 807 Ellis (Polk/Van Ness), 885-0725. 11am-9pm except Sunday. Once proclaimed as the best lowpriced Thai restaurant in town but I found it wanting. Spicy-sour soup with prawns $3.95, fish & noodle meat-ball soup $2.95, curry of day $3.35, chicken with garlic sauce $3.55, beef with bitter lemon $3.45, squid with chili pepper & bamboo shoots $3.50, fried whole fish $3.75-$4.60. ***(9)

ISLAND'S DELIGHT (Chinese), 1305 Polk (Bush), 474-6407. 11am-9pm Mon-Sat. Hot-sour soup $2.75, curry shrimp $4.25, beef with tender green $3.75, sweet-sour chicken $3.75, spareribs with bell pepper $3.65. ***(10)

PETE'S DELI & CAFE (Mideastern), 1661 Sutter (Divisadero), 931-4800. 7am-7pm Mon-Fri, 9am-5pm Sat. Chef salad $2.75, humus

$1.95, shrimp (1/2 pint) $2.95, baklava 85 cents, apple turnover $1.
***(11)

ALEXANDRIA CAFE (Mideastern), 508 Haight (Fillmore), 552-7390. 6:30 am-6pm, Sat-Sun 7am-2pm. A daily special $2.95, e.g., 1/2 BBQ chicken with salad & bread, lasagna with salad & bread, or quiche with salad. Mid-east combo-plate $3.95--humus, taboulah, falafel, tahini, feta cheese etc. Espresso 75 cents. ***(14)

ALL YOU KNEAD (Continental), 1466 Haight (Ashbury),552-4550. Quesadilla (salsa & jack cheese on a tortilla, topped with sour cream, guacamole and jalapenos) $4.10-$4.35. Quiche (spinach & mushroom or broccoli & cheddar) with salad $4.95. Linguine with meat sauce $4.25, or with mushroom-cashew stroganoff $4.50. Also serve a complete line of pizzas and calzones. ***(14)

CORDON ROUGE (Vietnamese), 1538 Haight (Ashbury/Clayton), 861-1812. 11am-10pm, Mon 6-10pm. Lunch, 11am-3pm --6 pot stickers $2.50; rice dishes with chicken, pork, imperial rolls etc. $2.75-$2.95. Dinner, with soup or salad & rice--charbroiled beef $4.75, 1/2 five-spice roast chicken $4.50, pork chops and chicken salad $4.25. ***(14)

PALL MALL GRILL (American), 1568 Haight (Ashbury/Clayton), 621-5877. 7am-8pm. Breakfast all day: eggs, fries, toast, coffee $2.50. 1/2-lb charbroiled burger $3.50, home fries $1. 1/4-lb burger $2.50. Spaghetti with meatsauce or pesto $3.75, veal parmigiana with spaghetti or salad $4.95, rib-eye steak and spaghetti $4.75, chicken stew $2. ***(14)

KUM LING (Chinese), 621 Clement (6 Av), 754-9520. 9am-9pm. Hot-sour soup $3.95, vegetables deluxe $3.50, lemon chicken $4.55, Szechuan beef $4.95, spareribs clay pot $4.50, mandarin duck $4.75. ***(22)

SKYDRAGON (Vietnamese), 914 Clement (10/11 Avs), 752-7480. 11am-2am. Sour soup with shrimp or fish $3.95, pork in clay pot $4.25, lemon grass chicken $4.75, 8 vegetables with pork $4.75, fried bananas in rum sauce $1.30. ***(22)

KUM MOON (Chinese), 2109 Clement (22nd Av), 221-5656. 11am-9:30pm. Mushu pork $4.25, lemon chicken $4.95, spareribs with pineapple $4.95, hot-sour soup $3. Dim sum combination plate $2.25 (4 items), $3.25 (5 items). ***(22)

HAMBURGER HAVEN (American), 800 Clement (9th Ave.), 387-3260. 7am-11pm daily, 1/2-lb hamburger with fries and vegetable $3.95; salad bar (seconds) included with sandwich or entree, e.g., turkey sandwich $2.95, club steak and fries $3.95. With soup or salad: liver/onions $4.50, breaded veal cutlet $4.50, halibut $5.75. ***(22)

BIG JOE'S BROILER, 2132 Irving (22/23 Avs), 731-5300. 7:30am-4:30pm. Sandwiches from $1.35 (cheese). Lunch specials--pork chops $3.95, liver/onions $3.85, rib-eyesteak & fries $5.20, fries 65 cents, ice cream 65 cents. Simple but clean counter-service. ***(20)

TAKEYA (Japanese), 5850 Geary Blvd (22 Av), 386-2777. 11am-9:30pm Mon-Fri, 5-9:30pm Sat, closed Sun. Lunch, including soup, pickle, rice, green tea--chicken teriyaki $4.10, tuna teriyaki $4.60, pork cutlet & egg $4.50, turbot in Japanese sauce $4.60, sashimi (raw tuna) $4.85. Beef & noodles $3.95, tempura with noodles $4.25. ***(13)

CAFE RUSSART (Russian), 6314 Geary Blvd (27 Av), 386-0180. 11am-8pm, closed Mon-Tues. Piroshki $1.30, pelmeni $2.50-$4.50, borsht $1.30 cup, $2.15 bowl. Veal stew $4.60-$5.60, green salad $1.25, tea 50 cents, pastries $1.10-$1.40. Intimate Russian tea room. ***(13)

SUM'S, 2450 Noriega (21/22 Sts), 665-6603. Entree includes soup or salad & fries--hamburger steak $4.25, pork chops $4.25, T-bone or sirloin steak $5.50. ***(20)

HAMBURGERS

Hamburgers are associated with fast-food chains. But there are a number of special hamburger restaurants that pride themselves on their individual style. Some grind the chuck before your eyes, while others have special charcoal broilers. Of course, they are more expensive than McDonald's but also much better. In my Lunch and Dinner listings, some hamburger offers are described. In this section, I will concentrate on restaurants that *feature* hamburgers, particularly the 1/2 pounders (which, with fries, make a meal). In ordering, be sure to specify rare, medium-rare or well-done and try to get one that is charcoal-broiled.

BEST BUY****

ORIGINAL JOE'S, 144 Taylor (Eddy) 775-4877, 1O:30-1am. For my money, the best value in town. Chuck is fresh-ground. 12-oz (yes, 3/4-pounder!) with thick fries, charbroiled after 5pm, $5. ****BEST BUY(1)

THE WHITE HORSE, 637 Sutter (Mason/Taylor), 771-1708. 7am-2:15pm Mon-Fri. Charbroiled hamburger (1/2-lb) and fries $4.75, available at lunch (11:30-2.15pm), including salad cart. This is one of the best values in town. ****BEST BUY(1)

POLO'S, 34 Mason (Market/Eddy), 362-7719, 11am-11pm Mon-Sat. 1/2-lb hamburger, fries $4.75; 16-oz. hamburger steak, vegetables and fries, $7.50: Charbroiled after 5pm. ****BEST BUY(1)

PAPA JOE'S, 1412 Polk (Pine), 441-2115. 7am-3pm Mon-Fri, to 2pm Sat, closed Sun. 1/3-lb hamburger with fries $2.35, 1/2-lb $2.95. ****BEST BUY(10)

BURGERVILLE, 1639 Polk (Clay/ Sacramento), 474-2280. 10:30am-9pm except Sun. 1/3-lb with steak fries $2.75. Hot sandwich with steak fries, cheese & avocado $2.60, ham & cheese $2.95. Soup 75 cents. ****BEST BUY(10)

LIPP'S, 201 9th St (Howard), 552-3466. Lunch 11am-3pm Mon-Fri, dinner 6-10pm Thurs-Sat. 1/2-lb hamburger with fries $4.95, salad $1.95, soups $1.95. ****BEST BUY(7)

HAMURGER MARY'S ORGANIC GRILL, 1582 Folsom (12 St), 626-5767. 10am-1am. A place with atmosphere, the more so as it gets late. 1/3-lb hamburgers start at $3.95. ***BEST BUY(7)

JAY N'BEE CLUB, 2736 20th St.(York), 648-0518. Lunch: 11am-2:30pm Mon-Fri. This is also a bar, serving lunch only, otherwise open all hours. The 1/2-lb hamburger comes with soup, butter and cheese, pasta or salad, *and* a small bottle of wine--all for $4.50. There is also ribeye steak on the full menu for $5.25 and N.Y.steak for $7.50. Crowded pub atmosphere, simple setting, good food. Be prepared for a wait. ****BEST BUY(17)

BALBOA CAFE, 3199 Fillmore (Greenwich), 921-3944. 11am-2am. Charbroiled 1/2-lb with fries $5.75. A little above our $5 range but worth it. ****BEST BUY(6)

MULHERN'S, 3635 Buchanan (opposite Safeway), 346-3635. 11:30am-10pm. 1/2-lb with fries $4.80. A recent "test" called it "the best in the Bay Area". ****BEST BUY(6)

ORIGINAL JOE'S No. 2, corner Chestnut & Fillmore, 346-3233. No relation to the one on Taylor St. (above). 1:30pm-1am. 12-oz with fries $4.95; hamburger steak with fries, spaghetti ravioli or vegetable $8.45. Menu is a clone of the Taylor St restaurant but prices are generally higher. ****BEST BUY(6)

GOOSE LAKE TAVERN, 3345 Steiner (Lombard/Chestnut), 563-4173. 11:30am-10:30pm, Sat-Sun from 9:30am. Charbroiled, 1/2-lb with fries $4.95. ****BEST BUY(6)

ORPHAN ANDY'S, 3991 17th St. (Market/Castro), 864-9795. Open 24 hours every day. 1/2-lb charbroiled with fries $3.65. ****BEST BUY(15)

WITHOUT RESERVATION, 460 Castro (18/Market), 861-9510. 7:30am-2:30am. Charbroiled 1/2-lb cheeseburger with fries $5.50. Dinner with soup or salad, 1/2-lb hamburger steak with mushrooms $5.95, grilled liver & onions $5.85, BBQ pork ribs in honey sauce $6.95. Bowl soup $1.60, mixed salad $1.85. Wine liter $4.95. ****BEST BUY(15)

WELCOME HOME, 464 Castro (18/ Market), 626-3600. 7:30am-10pm. Charbroiled, 1/2-lb $3.25, French fries & soft drink add 60 cents. With cole slaw--6oz rib eye steak sandwich $5.75, seafood sandwich $3.75. Dinners from 5pm, with soup or salad--broiled pork chops $5.95, meat loaf $5.25, breast of chicken dijon $5.45. Wine liter $4. ****BEST BUY(15)

IRVING CLUB, 2328 Irving (24/25 Avs), 731-2580. 10am-2am. Bar-restaurant. 1/2-lb with fries $3.95. ****BEST BUY(20)

951 CLEMENT, 951 Clement (12 Av), 387-3555. 5-10pm. Charbroiled, 10oz with chips $4.75. Elegant. ****BEST BUY(22)

THE COURTYARD, 2436 Clement (25/26 Avs), 387-7616. 11:30am-2:30pm & 5-9:30pm. 10-oz, charbroiled, with fries $5.25. ****BEST BUY(23)

SIMPLE(*)--VERY GOOD(***)

TAD'S, 120 Powell (Ellis), 982-1718. 7am-8pm. Charbroiled hamburger with baked potato & salad $2.49. ***(9)

BIG HORN, 808 Geary (Hyde), 776-5619. 12 noon to midnight. Charbroiled 1/2-lb with fries $3.05. Hamburger steak, with soup & salad, coffee or tea, $6. ***(1)

GEARY STEAK HOUSE, 901 Geary (Larkin), 776-6300. Cafeteria. 11am-11pm. 6-oz with salad & fries $3.25; 10-oz hamburger plate with salad, baked potato & garlic bread $5.50. All charbroiled. ***(1)

THE FRONT ROOM, 1500 California (Polk/Larkin), 771-1591. See phonebook for other locations. 11am-midnight. 1/3-lb, charbroiled, with soup, salad or fries $3.95, 1/2-pounder $4.25. ***(10)

BOB'S BROILER, 1601 Polk (Sacramento), 474-6161. 8am-11pm. 1/2-lb with potato salad or fries, charbroiled, $3.65. Soup & sandwich $2.95. Seafood dinners, with soup or salad, trout $5.95, rib-eye steak $5.35. ***(10)

SUGAR BROILER, corner Fillmore & Sacramento, 922-4199. Cafeteria-style. 11am-5pm Mon-Fri. 1/4-lb $1.99-2.35, fries 79 cents, green salad 75 cents. Fish & chips $1.99, chicken nuggets & fries $2.95. Coffee, tea 40 cents. ***(11)

THE GOLD POST, 2700 16 St. (Harrison), 552-4290. Cafeteria. 6am-3:30pm Mon-Fri, Sat 7am-2pm. 1/2-lb with fries $2.75, charbroiled. ***(16)

PERSIS CAFE (Italian, Persian), 248 Divisadero (Haight), 863-6558. Charbroiled, 1/2-lb with fries on torpedo bread $3.75. Also full Italian & Persian menus (see Intermediate Restaurants). ***(14)

JIM'S COUNTRY KITCHEN, 235 Church (Market), 621-3040. 6:30am-9:30pm.1/2-lb with fries $3.75. ***(15)

HOT'N HUNKY, 4039 18 St (Castro), 621-6365. 11:30am-11pm. 1/2-lb $3.29, 3/4-lb $3.89, fries 90 cents. ***(15)

BULLSHEAD, 3745 Geary Blvd (Arguello/2nd Av), 668-2323 and 840 Ulloa (West Portal), 665-4350. noon-10pm Mon-Sat, 4-11pm Sun. 1/2-lb with fries $3.45 (plus salad bar $1.95 additional). 1/2-lb ground sirloin, with soup or salad bar, $7.95. ***(13)(21)

BUN 'BURGER, 503 Clement (6 Av), 221-7768. 6am-6pm Mon-Sat.
1/3-lb with fries or potato salad $3.15, charbroiled on request.
***(22)

HAMBURGER HAVEN, 800 Clement (9 Av), 387-3260. 7am-
11pm. 1/2-lb with fries, vegetable & salad bar $3.95, charbroiled.
Fish & chips $3.75, spaghetti & meat balls with salad $3.95. ***(22)

BILL'S PLACE, 2315 Clement (24 Av), 221-5262. 11am-9pm. Very
popular. 5-oz $3.25-$4.60, fries $1 extra. Overpriced, but the 10-oz
hamburger with salad & fries for $6.20 is good value. ***(22)

Pizza

Pizza is an economical meal. 3-4 persons can dine well on an *extra-
large* $12-$14 (some are even cheaper) pizza. New pizza restau-
rants--some with Italian lunch and dinner menus, as well--open almost weekly in S.F. There are so many that it is possible to review
only a fraction. Here are some that I consider especially good. First, a
few definitions: *Neapolitan* is thin crust, *Sicilian* is thick-crust; some
restaurants offer both. *Calzone* is a folded-over or stuffed pizza
containing cheese, ham and often other ingredients. *Chicago-style* is a
deep-dish pizza. Sizes are usually referred to as *small, medium, large*
and *extra-large* and the meaning of these sizes often varies but *extra-
large* is usually 16" in diameter. As a rule, *medium* is often too much
for 2 and *extralarge* too much for 3.

BEST BUY****

BLONDIE'S, 63 Powell (Ellis), 982-6168. 11am-9pm, Sun to 7pm.
Huge slice 94 cents, with 1 topping $1.55, with 2 toppings $1,85,
with 3 toppings $2.11. 16oz soft drink 56 cents. You'll always see
mobs there, a good sign. ****(9)

GOLDEN BOY PIZZA, 542 Green (Columbus/Grant), 982-9738,
11am-midnight, closed Sun. Pizzas, slice, cheese, $1.50, combo
$1.75. Full sheet, 15 slices, 6x6", $22.50. Espresso 75 cents,
cappucino $1.25, beer 85 cents. Counter and tables. ****BEST
BUY(3)

PIZZERIA UNO, 2200 Lombard/Steiner) and 2323 Powell (Bay), 563-3144. 11:30am-12:30am, FriSat 1:30am. Chicago-style deepdish pizza. $2.35-$4.79 individual, *regular* for 2 $4.45-$9.50, *large* for 3-4 $7.95-$15.75. House salad--lettuce, green pepper, mushrooms, tomato--with dinner $1.75, meal size $3.25; Wine 1/2 liter $3.75, liter $6.75. Express Lunch--house salad or soup & individual pizza of day--$3.75. A favorite. ****BEST BUY(6)(4)

VILLAGE PIZZERIA, 3348 Steiner (Chestnut), 931-2470 and Van Ness (Sutter), 673-7771, 11am-11pm   daily. Slices--Neapolitan $1.10, Sicilian $1.25, 40 cents extra for topping. Neapolitan range from $7.50-$10 for 14" and $9-$12.25 for 16"; Sicilian range from $8-$12.25 for 1/2 and $12.75-$15 for a whole pizza. Wine 1/2 liter $3. liter $5. A favorite. ****BEST BUY (6)(10)

VICTOR'S, 1411 Polk (California/ Sacramento), 885-1660. Lunch 12-2pm, dinner 5-10pm. Range $4.50 (small)-$10.90 (extra large) vegetarian extralarge $10, calzone for 2-3 with salami or vegetarian $10. Pastas or ravioli, with or without meat balls, $4.70-$6, lasagna or canneloni $5.90. ****BEST BUY(10)

GIORGIO'S, 151 Clement (2 Ave), 668-1266, 11am-11:30pm. Pizzas range from 11"-17" size, from $5-$14.25. Calzone (stuffed pizza), depending on size and stuffing, $5.35-$11.70. Cannelloni, baked lasagne, or baked rigatoni $5.75. Pasta dishes $4.75-$5.75. **** BEST BUY (22)

RONNIES, 264 Church (15th/Market), 626-8666, 12 noon-1am, Fri-Sat to 2am. Pizzas range from $6 for 12" and $6.95-$8 for 16". Dinner entrees served with soup and salad--moussaka $6, veal scallopini $7.50, chicken cacciatore $7.50, N.Y.steak (16 oz) $9. ($7.50 a la carte) spaghetti & meat balls $5.60, lasagne or cannelloni $6. ****BEST BUY(15)

ROYAL KITCHEN, 3253 Mission (21 St), 824-4219, 11am-9pm except Tues and Sun. 3-9pm. This a Chinese restaurant that harbored an acclaimed Italian pizza section and then took over when the Italian pizza-maker left. They now make the entire Italian range plus an interesting Chinese version of their own. Price range $6.25-$13.25. Try the pesto or garlic for Italian, also the Chinese variety. Well worth a visit. A favorite. ****BEST BUY(16)

VERY GOOD***

CALIFORNIA PIZZA, 1534 California (Polk/Larkin), 775-2525, 11am-1am, Mon-Fri. 12" $4.55, 16" $7.20. Also submarines, 10" on French bread $3.15, pastas with soup or salad $5.75. Wine $5.50 bottle. ***(10)

PIZZA PANTRY, 1725 Polk (Clay), 441-3137, 11:30am-midnight daily. Range $4.25-$12. Spaghetti or ravioli and meat balls with fresh bread and butter $4.95; lasagna $4.95, salad (make your own) $1.75, 1/2 liter wine $3.15, liter $5.25. ***(10)

THE FRONT ROOM, 1500 California (Polk/Larkin), 771-1591, 4am-midnight, Fri-Sat to 2am. Two other locations: 823 Clement (9th Ave), 387-7733 and 1385 9th Ave. (Judah), 665-2900. Pizza: just cheese $3.55-$10.10 (16"). Deepdish pizza $7.30-$16.90. Italian dinners include soup or salad, garlic bread and ice cream--lasagna or cannelloni $6.95, ravioli or spaghetti $6.95, veal parmignani or scallopini $8.95. ***(10)

BROADWAY PIZZA, 760 Broadway (Powell/Stockton), 788-8555. 11am1pm and 5pm-1am Mon-Thurs, 11am-3am Fri-Sun. Small $5.10-$8.10, extra-large $8.50-$12.10. With salad--spaghetti or ravioli & meat balls $5.95, whole chicken $6.95, eggplant parmesan $4.95, pitcher draft beer $3.95. ***(3)

NORTH BEACH PIZZA, 1499 Grant Av (Union), 433-2444. 11am-1am, Fri-Sat to 3am. Small $3.65-$6.35, extra-large $6.60-$8.90. Spaghetti with meat balls, soup & salad $5.50, canneloni $6.05. Entrees with soup or salad, vegetables, spaghetti, bread & butter--veal scallopini $7.50, T-bone steak $8.60, chicken cacciatore $7.55, prawns $8.75. ***(3)

DE PAULA'S, (Brazilian food, pizza), 2114 Fillmore (California), 346-9888, 5-11:30pm MonTues, Fri-Sat to 1am. Italian pizza and Brazilian specialties, e.g., feijoada completa $10.30. Pizzas range from $3.55 (7") to $15.80 (16"). Dinners with soup or salad--veal piccata $8.95, veal parmigiano $8.95. Also, spaghetti, fettucini, ravioli $5.40-$6.70. Phone for Brazilian specialties. ***(11)

PAULINE'S PIZZA, 260 Valencia (14 St), 552-2050. 3-10pm Wed-Sat. Range from $6.75 (small) to $13.50 (extra large), specialties: pesto, garlic or andouille sausage pizzas. Used to be housed in Royal Kitchen on Mission (see above). ***(16)

DIM SUM

Dim Sum includes many Chinese delicacies that, combined, make an excellent lunch, e.g., shrimp dumplings, pork buns, meat turnovers, wrapped chicken, spareribs. A waiter or waitress comes by every few minutes, and you can choose a dish, usually with 3 items on it. Later, the plates are tallied up, and you pay according to the number of plates you have accumulated. Two or three persons can have a good lunch for $3-$4 per person, depending on the price per dish. Remember, there is a charge for tea, usually around $1 per person, unless otherwise indicated.

BEST BUY****

GRAND PALACE, 859 Grant (Washington/Jackson), 982-3705, 9am-3pm daily. $1.35 per dish. A favorite. **** BEST BUY(2)

TUNG FONG, 808 Pacific (Stockton), 362-7115. 9am-3pm daily, except Wed. $1.35 a dish. A favorite. ****BEST BUY(2)

ASIA GARDEN, 722 Pacific (Grant), 398-5112. 9-2:30pm, $1.35 per dish. ****BEST BUY(2)

KING OF CHINA, 939 Clement (9am-10pm), 668-2618. $1.44 per dish. Also, full Chinese menu. One critic considers this the best dim sum in the U.S.; many agree it is probably the best in the Bay Area. There is a famous branch in Hong Kong. ****BEST BUY(22)

THE FOOK RESTAURANT, 332 Clement (4th Ave.), 668-8070. $1.35 per dish. Also full Chinese menu. ****BEST BUY(22)

ROYAL KITCHEN, 3253 Mission (29 St), 824-4219. 11am-9pm, 3-9pm Tues & Sun. $1.75, large portions and *no tea-service charge*. Also, full Chinese menu. ****BEST BUY(16)

VERY GOOD***

CANTON TEA HOUSE, 1108 Stockton (Jackson), 982-1030, 7:30am-4pm, $1.45 per dish. ***(2)

HANG AH TEA ROOM, 1 Hang Ah St.(Off Sacramento near Stockton). 982-5686, 10am-9pm Tues-Sun. Dim sum plate for one person: seven items, $3.65; dinner, including egg roll, fried prawns, fish ball, shrimp toast, parchment chicken, $5. Per dish $1.35. Also, full Chinese menu. ***(2)

YANK SING, 427 Battery (Washington), 362-1640. 11am-3pm Mon-Fri, 10am-4pm Sat and Sun. $1.80-$2.15 per dish. Probably the most expensive dim sum in San Francisco. ***(2)

KUM SHAN, 3011 Fillmore (Filbert), 567-3066, lunch 11:30am-2:30pm, dinner 5-10pm, Tues-Sun; 5-10pm Sat. $1.40 per dish. Also, full Chinese menu. ***(6)

Sushi

Sushi--basically raw fish filets, usually wrapped in a special "vinegar rice" or served over the sushi-rice--has been around for about 100 years but only recently has it exploded into a national pastime. Almost every Japanese restaurant now serves sushi and sushi bars devoted solely to sushi have sprung up everywhere, some mere holes-in-the-wall. The quality of sushi depends on the choice of the freshest possible fish and the preparation of the vinegar-rice. The large restaurants have their own sushi-chefs and strive for quality ingredients but they are usually expensive. The trick is to find sushi-bars that know their business, use quality products and are reasonably priced. If you have the time, a visit to Japantown--Post Street from Laguna to Sutter, where the 2-Clement, 4-Sutter and 3-Jackson buses run--would be a good place to seek out your sushi. There are 1/2 dozen or more sushi-bars and restaurants, some of whom display their wares or photos at the entrance.

But, let's face it, sushi is not a poor man's dish. Here is a list of some sushi bars and restaurants--some are combined with tempura specialties that are reasonably-priced. An asterisk(*) indicates restaurant is also recommended for Japanese food other than sushi.

*GLOBUS WEST, 419 Grant (Bush), 982-3656. 11-2:30pm Mon-Sat, 6-9pm daily. (2)

SUSHI-ON-THE-ROCKS, 500 Broadway (Kearny/Grant), 362-6434 and 1475 Polk (California), 441-6854. 30-40 varieties. The Broadway restaurant also has a hot menu. Both feature all-you-can-eat specials, $6.95 for lunch & $8.95 for dinner, featured as "the best price for sushi in the U.S.". (3)(10)

ISO BUNE, 1737 and 1684 (Post (Japantown), 563-1030 and 563-4486. 11:30am-10pm daily, appears on little boats; you take your pick, like choosing dim sum. (12)

*MIFUNE, Restaurant Mall Japantown, 922-0337. 11am-9pm daily. (12)

*OTAFUKU-TEI, 1737 Buchanan (Japantown), 931-1578. 5-10pm Mon-Sat. (12)

INO SUSHI, Japantown, 1620 Webster, 922-3121. 5:30-10.30pm Tues-Sat. Very small bar with only 8 seats at counter and 2 small tables. (12)

*SANPPO, 1702 Post (Buchanan/Japantown), 346-3486. 11:45am-3pm and 5:30pm-10.30pm Tues-Sat, 3-10pm Sun. (12)

OSOME, 1923 Fillmore (Pine), 346-2311. 5-11pm, closed Tues. (11)

*TEN ICHI, 2225 Fillmore (Clay), 346-3477. 11:30-2pm Mon-Fri, 5-10pm Sat. (11)

SUSHI DELIGHT, 1800 Divisadero (corner Bush) 931-1773, 11:30-2pm Mon-Fri, 5:30pm-10:30pm Mon-Sat. (11)

*TOYO, 3226 Geary (Spruce/ Parker), 387-6564. (13)

EBISU, 1283 9th Ave. (Lincoln/Irving) 566-1770. 11:30am-2:30pm Mon-Fri, 5-10pm Mon-Sat. (19)

HAPPI SUSHI, 5041 Geary Blvd. (17 Av), 221-6210, 5-10pm. except Mon. (19)

LADY SEIKKO'S, 2154 Mission (18th/19th Sts.), 558-8246, 11:30am-10pm except Sat:4.30-10pm. Closed Sun. (16)

Fish & Chips

EDNA'S ENGLISH FISH & CHIPS, 309 Columbus (Broadway), 781-7369. 11:30am-11pm, Mon-Sat, 12-9pm Sun. One piece codfish & chips $2.25, 2 pieces $3.55, 3 pieces $3.95. Fishburger $1.50, beer $1-$1.60, coffee 50 cents, coleslaw 40 cents. ****BEST BUY(3)

THE OLD CHELSEA, 932 Larkin (Post/Geary), 474-5015. 4-10pm daily. English type fish and chips 2 pieces $2.95, 1/2 order $2.20, prawns & chips $4.80, chips only $1.25. A favorite. ****BEST BUY(1)

PICADILLY, 1348 POLK (Pine), 771-6477. 11am-11pm Mon-Fri, to 1am Sat-Sun. Special: 1 piece fish, chips, onion rings $1.40 (terrific value). Two pieces $2.90, 3 pieces $3.60. Also chicken and chips $3.50, crab and chips $4.15. ****BEST BUY(10)

DUBLIN, 4326 Geary (7th Ave), 387-3800. 11:30am-10pm Mon-Sat, 1-10pm Sun. One piece fish and chips $2, 2 pieces $2.90, 3 pieces $3.80. Eggplant or zucchini $1. A favorite. ****BEST BUY(13)

VERY GOOD***

UNION JACK FISH & CHIPS, 350 Bay (North Point/North Point Mall) 989-6532. 9:30am-7pm daily. One piece fish and chips $1.79, 2 pieces $2.59, family portion for 3 $7.99. Coney island clam chowder 75 cents and $1.45, 2 pieces chicken, chips and coleslaw $2.50, 3 pieces $2.85. ***(4)

LONDON FISH & CHIPS, 225 Clement (3rd Ave), 752-8481. 10:30am-10pm Mon-Sat and 1-9:30pm Sun. Full order (2 pieces fish and chips) $3.15, 1/2 order (1 piece) $2.15; full order prawns and chips $4.35, half-order $2.99; clams and chips $2.65. ***(22)

Fast Foods

Like all major cities, San Francisco abounds in fast food establishments, many of which are in the downtown area. Here is a list of the major ones, the addresses of which can be found in the white or yellow pages of the phone-book. Attention is especially called to the salad bars at *Burger King*, *Carl's Jr.*, *Wendy's* and *Round Table Pizza*.

BURGER KING
CARL'S JR.
CHURCH FRIED CHICKEN
DONUTS & THINGS
INTERNATIONAL HOUSE OF PANCAKES
JACK-IN-the-BOX
KENTUCKY FRIED CHICKEN
McDONALD'S
PIONEER (FRIED CHICKEN)
POPEYE CHICKEN. One critic considers this the best of the chicken fast-foods.
ROUND TABLE PIZZA
H.SALT ESQ. FISH & CHIPS
VIKING GIANT SUBMARINES
WENDY'S OLD FASHIONED HAMBURGERS
WINCHELL'S DONUTHOUSE

VI. Intermediate Restaurants $5-$10 Per Person

Ethnic Restaurants

BEST BUY****

LA QUICHE (French), 550 Taylor (Geary/Post), 441-2711. 11:30am-2:30pm & 5:30-10pm. Crepes with salad--Swiss cheese, eggs & ham $5.95; creamed spinach, eggs & ham $6.25, crab meat with cream sauce $7.15. Dinners with soup, salad and vegetables--beef bourgignon $9.95, veal marengo $10.25, catch of day with garlic butter $9.95. Small, elegant. ****BEST BUY(1)

SWISS ALPS (Swiss), 605 Post (Taylor), 885-0947. 5-10 Tues.-Sat. Dinner entrees include souptca *and* salad, e.g., bratwurst $7.75, sweetbreads with mushrooms in cream & brandy sauce $9.95, sauerbraten with German noodles $10.45, cheese fondue (specialty) for 2 $16, beef fondue (specialty) for 2 $26. ****BEST BUY(1)

THE WHITE HORSE (American), 637 Sutter (Mason/Taylor), 771-1708, 7am-10:45am and 11:30am-2:15pm Mon-Fri. Lunch includes salad cart (seconds), e.g., hamburger 1/2-lb, (charbroiled) and fries $4.75, fish (catch of the day) $5.75, veal cutlet $4.75. Salad cart alone (all-you-can-eat) $3.70. Cheese cake $1.25, coffee 65 cents, liter of wine $4.75. Elegant restaurant, part of Beresford Hotel. Excellent value, considering salad cart. ****BEST BUY(1)

ATHENS GREEK RESTAURANT, 39 Mason (Market), 775-1929, 11am-10pm. Mon-Sat. Counter, small tables, no-nonsense food atmosphere, wholesome, tasty Greek food. Lamb dishes, vegetables $5.75, mousaka $5.75, stuffed eggplant $4.35, calamari $5.50. Lemon soup with meal $1, salad with meal $1.50. ****BEST BUY(9)

GERMAN COOK, 612 O'Farrell (Jones), 776-9022, 4:30-9:30pm Tues-Sat. Menu changes daily, all items a la carte. Entree served with potatoes and red cabbage or vegetable. Bratwurst or knockwurst $4.95, sauerbraten $6.95, wienerschnitzel $7.95, 1/2 roast duck $7.95. ****BEST BUY(9)

LIPP'S (Continental), 201 9th St. (Howard), 552-3466. 6-10pm Tues-Thurs. Entrees served with soup or salad--fettucine Alfredo or linguine $5.95, coq au vin $5.95, goulash $5.95. ****BEST BUY(7)

MEKONG (Vietnamese), 730 Larkin (Ellis/O'Farrell), 9am-9pm, 928-8989. Beef noodle soup $22.95, fried prawns sweet-sour $4.75, coconut chicken in lemon-grass & coconut sauce $3.95, 5-spice BBQ beef $4.25, sauteed pork & vegetables $4.25. Beef Dinner Special for 2--$14.95, 7 beef dishes, including beef fire-pot, BBQ beef, grilled beef. ****BEST BUY(9)

RAFFLES (Polynesian), 1390 Market (Hayes), 621-8601. 11am-10pm Mon-Sat. Dinner includes Pu-Pu's (crab, pork, (crab, pork, zucchini), soup or salad--chicken sesame $8.95, curry prawns $9.95, teriyaki steak $9.95, pineapple chicken $8.50, BBQ ribs $7.50.A la carte--sirloin steak sandwich with fries & salad $5.95, hunan beef $7.50, seafood salad (crab & shrimp) $7.95, sweet-sour prawns $8.50. avocado-bacon cheeseburger with fries & salad $5.50. ****BEST BUY(7)

NOB HILL NOSHERY (Continental), 1400 Pacific (Hyde), 928-6674. 7am-11pm. Delirestaurant. Baked brie with French bread $4.50, pate & cheese plate $4.95, salami & cheese $3.95. Entrees, served with salad--pork chop & rice $6.95, BBQ chicken & rice $5.95, Lasagne $6.95, chicken parmesan & spaghetti $6.95, jambalaya shrimp, chicken & rice $7.95. ****BEST BUY(10)

LA CUISINE CAFE (French), 1555 Pacific Ave. (Polk/Larkin), 441-3548. Appetizers are high but can be shared--escargots $4.50, quiche Lorraine $5.75, liver pate $5.25. Pasta (can also be shared)--fettucine provencale $5.75, Alfredo $5.95. Entrees--red snapper provencale $7, filet petrale almandine $7.50, chicken breast tarragon $7.50, lamb brochette $8.95, prawns in garlic butter $9.50, veal champagne $9.95, streak Diane $10.50. Chocolate mousse (recommended) $2.25. Espresso 95 cents, capuccino $1.25. Excellent wines, including a French Beaujolais, $10. (No wonder, the waiter is an acknowledged lecturer on wines!). ****(10)

LABODEGA (Spanish), 1337 Grant Ave. (North Beach), 433-0439. Wed-Sun evenings. One dish only--paella, $11. Flamenco dancing, Fridays classical guitar. ****BEST BUY(3)

MAKADEH (Persian), 470 Green Street (Grant Av), 362-8286. 12 noon-11pm Tues-Sun. Yoghourt with cucumbers (served with hot pita bread) is a good appetizer for 2--$1.95, as are stuffed grape leaves $2.50; barley & vegetable soup $2. All guests receive an opening dish with feta cheese, scallions, onions and mint leaves, with pita bread; it comes with meal. Entrees, served with safron rice--skewered mixture of ground lamb & beef $5.95, skewered slices of beef $7.95, shish kebab $8.95, chicken marinated in yoghourt $7.50, lamb shank cooked in onions, scallions, leeks, beans etc. $7.50. Rose-petal flavored ice cream $2.50. Wine 1/2 liter $3.75, liter $6.95 (burgundy is excellent and goes well with lamb). All meats are marinated for about 3 days in lemon juice, saffron and spices. Restaurant is elegant (cloth tablecloth & napkins, fresh flowers. Worth a visit. ****BEST BUY(4)

IL POLLAIO, 555 Columbus Ave (Washington Square), 362--7727. 11:30am-9pm, closed Tues. All meats served with salad--chicken, flattened & grilled, 1/2 $3.50, whole $6.95; veal t-bone steak $8.50, beef or pork ribs $8.50, lamb chop $5.85. Daily specials, with salad & bread--3 pieces chicken $4.25; 1/2 chicken $4.95, 2 Italian sausages $3.50, 5-oz hamburger & fries $4.25. Fri-Sat-Sun Special--1/2 rabbit with salad or fries $9.50. Bowl soup with meals $1.50. Excellent grills. ****BEST BUY(4)

PERSIS CAFE (Italian, Persian), 248 Divisadero (Haight), 863-6558. 11am-10pm. Italian menu includes: spaghetti & meat balls $5.75, fettucine alfredo $5.25, linguini with wine sauce $7.50, veal scallopini $7.50. Persian entrees are served with feta cheese & pita bread; entrees also include rice, tomatoes & onions--chicken kebab $6.25, lamb kebab $6.95, ground beef & lamb $5.75, filet mignon $7.25. Persian meats are marinated in lemon juice, onions & saffron. Interesting combination of menus. ****BEST BUY(14)

GLADWIN'S (International, mesquite grill), 2217 Market (Noe/Castro), 624-9204. 5-10 Tues-Sun. Entrees served with soup or salad, vegetables, rice or fries--snapper with pepper sauce $8.50, seabass with basil & garlic sauce $9.50, monkfish with lemon & tarragon $9.50, lamb chop $12.50, kashmir chicken with curry $7.95, chicken diavolo $8.75, snapper Moroccan-style $7.95. Also, Greek dishes. Elegant, excellent grills. ****BEST BUY(15)

DUO (International), 4094 18th St (Castro), 552-8388. 5-10pm Mon-Sat, Sun from noon. With soup or salad--Jambalaya (Creole) $8.95, feijada (Brazilian) $8.95, eggplant parmigiana $5.25, egg pie with spinach & cheese $5.25, lasagna $6.75, riccota-stuffed meatloaf $6.95. A la carte--veal parmigiana $6.95, chicken cordon bleu (with cheese & ham). Greek dinner with soup & dessert $9.50, mousaka $6.95. Turn-of-century decor. ****BEST BUY(16)

GLOBOS (Japanese), 419 Grant (Bush), 982-3656. 11:30am-2:30pm & 6:30-9:30pm. Lunch--including rice, soup & pickles--sesame chicken & green salad $4.50, beef teriyaki $5.75, sukiyaki $6, pork rib $5.25. Dinner--including appetizer, rice, soup, pickles--75 cents more than lunch. Ice cream 70 cents, Kirin beer $1.40. ****BEST BUY(1)

SUN HUNG YUEN (Chinese), 744 Washington (Grant/Kearny), 982-2319. 11:30am-midnight, closed Tues. Egg flower soup $2, almond chicken $4, mandarin duck $4.50, prawns with cashew nuts $5.75, beef with ginger $5.50, sweet-sour pork $4.50. One of Chinatown's oldest and best. A favorite. ****BEST BUY(2)

KING TIN (Chinese), 826 Washington (Grant/Stockton), 982-8228. Won ton soup $2.10, roast duck $4, BBQ pork $4, sweet-sour fish $5, spicy shrimp $6.50, beef with vegetables $4.50, orange juice spareribs $4.50, sizzling shrimp $7.50, sizzling chicken $5, clay pots $4-$5.50. Congee (Chinese rice-porridge) $2.30-$3.70. ****BEST BUY(2)

POT STICKER (Chinese), 150 Waverly Place (Grant/Stockton), 397-9985. 11:30am-9:45pm. 4 Pot stickers $1.85, 6 $3.15. Hot-sour soup $3.15, mandarin or twice-cooked pork $4.95, green onion or broccoli beef $5.55, garlic or lemon chicken $5.25, assorted vegetables $4.25, Szechuan prawns $6.75. ****BEST BUY (2)

CHUNG KING (Chinese), 606 Jackson (Grant/Kearny), 963-3899. 11:30am-9:30pm. Hot-sour soup for 3-4 $3.25, almond or cashew chicken $4.95, ginger beef $4.95, sweet-sour spareribs $4.95, curry or mongolian beef $4.95, black bean sauce shrimp $5.95, cashew nut shrimps $5.95, vegetables deluxe $3.95. Rice flour steamed pork or spareribs (house special) $3.95. Interesting dinner menus for $6 & $8 per person, minimum 2. ****BEST BUY(2)

OCEAN SKY (Chinese), 641 Jackson (Grant/Kearny), 433-6802. 11am-3am. Hot-sour soup $4, hot pots $4.50-$5.25, e.g., beef stew or sizzling chicken, cashew chicken $4.75, sweet-sour pork $4.75, prawns with cashew $6, curry beef $4.75, vegetables deluxe $4.25. Also, porridge dishes (9pm-3am) $2.50-$3. ****BEST BUY(2)

YUET LEE (Chinese), 1300 Stockton (Broadway), 982-6020. 9am-2am, except Tues. Top restaurant critics continue to call this one of the very best in the Bay Area but one critic warns, correctly, that the special fish dishes can be overly expensive, therefore stick to the dishes on the printed menu. In this way, a party of 4 or 5 can easily put a Family Dinner together (1 soup and 1 dish per person, plus rice) for $6-$8 per person, e.g., mixed-ingredients soup $3.95, sizzling spareribs (clay pot) $4.25, braised sea eel with pork & garlic (clay pot) $5.25, beef with cashews $4.25, sweet-sour pork $3.25, mixed vegetables $3.75, prawns chow mein $4.75, porridge dishes $2.25-$3.75. A favorite. ****BEST BUY(2)

HUNAN VILLAGE (Chinese), 839 Kearny (Columbus), 956-7868 & 272 Sutter (Stockton/Grant), 433-7878. 11am-9:30pm, to 10pm Fri-Sat. An East-Coast critic called this the best Chinese restaurant in the USA. Potstickers $2.95, shrimp rolls $2.50, hot-sour or seafood soup $3.95, hot pepper chicken $4.95, Hunan twice-cooked pork $5.25, beef with celery or green pepper $5.75, sweet-sour ribs $5.25, sizzling shrimp $6.50, 3-ingredients seafood $6.50, smoked or crispy tea duck (1/2) $8.50. Also Lunch menu with dishes $3.25-$3.95, over noodles or rice. ****BEST BUY(1)

PEPPINO'S (Italian), 1247 Polk (Bush/Sutter), 11am-10pm. Gnocchi with pesto $6.75, fettucine with meat balls $6.95, calamari saute with linguine $7.95, chicken cacciatore $7.95, veal marsala $8.95, spaghetti $4.95, ravioli pesto $6.75, minestrone $1.95, dinner salad $1.95. Large portions, nice atmosphere, including sidewalk terrace. ****BEST BUY(10)

LA TRATTORIA (Italian), 1507 Polk (California), 771-6363. 11:30am-11:30pm Mon-Sat, 3-10:30pm Sun. Mixed green salad with olives & tomatoes $1.75, ministrone $1.75. Spaghetti carbonara $5.95, vongole $6.95, al pesto $5.95, canneloni with veal & cheese $6.95, hamburger & fries $3.75, calamari saute $7.95, veal marsala $8.95. Pleasant sidewalk terrace. ****BEST BUY(10)

TAI CHI (Chinese), 2031 Polk (Pacific/Broadway), 441-6758. Hunan-Mandarin cuisine. Hot-sour soup $2.95, curry beef $5.25, twice-cooked pork $4.95, sizzling shrimp $6.50, bean-sauce chicken $4.95, vegetables deluxe $4.50. Also, a number (15) of vegetarian dishes $3.95-$5.25. ****BEST BUY(10)

WATER LILY CAFE (Continental), 2400 Polk (Union), 673-9940. 9am-3pm and 5:30-10pm daily except Wed. Dinner is a la carte: Fettucine Alfredo $5.75, fettucine carbonara $6.75, chicken cacciatore $5.95, fresh fish of the day $6.50-$7, steak Dianne $8.95, sauteed scallops $8.45, chocolate mousse $1.75. ***(5)

XENIOS (Greek), 2237 Polk (Green), 775-2800. 5-10pm except Tues. Egg-lemon soup $1.75, tarama (creamy white caviar) $2.25, hot spinach-cheese pie $2.75, mixed cold plate (tarama, grape leaves & eggplant salad) $3.25. Fried calamari $6.75, marinated rabbit $8.50, stuffed roast duck in wine sauce $8.50 (house specialty), lamb saute with eggplant & cheese $8.25, 1/2 rack of lamb $10.75, prawns & scallops in white wine $9.75. Also pastas, e.g., fettucine with smoked ham $6.50 and Greek salad $2.50. You can make a wonderful meal of 2-3 appetizers and a bottle of wine. Elegant dining, a favorite. ****(10)

THE MAGIC GRILL (Vietnamese), 2348 Polk (at Union), 771-5544. 5:30-10:30pm daily. Entrees are served with soup or salad--filet sole meuniere $6.25, trout almadine $6.50,calamari with mushrooms, pepper & garlic $5.95, fisherman's platter deep fried $7.95, red snapper with pineapple $5.95, tea, coffee 60 cents. See also under Steaks. ****BEST BUY(10)

BEETHOVEN RESTAURANT (German), 1701Powell (Union/Columbus), 391-4488. 5:30-10:30pm Tues-Sat. Entrees served with soup *and* salad, e.g., bratwurst, red cabbage & potatoes $9.95, pork roast with red cabbage & potato pancakes $9.95, sauerbraten $11.40, Eisbein (boiled pickled joint) $9.90. Goulasch soup $1.50, Bismarck herring in sour cream with apples $4.75 (good appetizer for 2). Best German restaurant in town, also best potato pancakes. ****(BEST BUY(3)

PASAND (Indian-Madras), 1876 Union (Laguna), 922-4498. 11:30am-10pm. Thick lentil-vegetable soup $1.25, Indian breads $1-$1.50, yogurt with cucumbers & sauces $1.25. Complete Thali dinner is $8.50-$11 (price is determined by the entree) and includes choice of entree (vegetable curry, curry lamb, chicken cooked with yogurt, curry shrimp etc.), lentil curry, thick lentil vegetable soup, mango chutney, lentil wafer, deep-fried Indian bread, rice pilaf & dessert. Entrees alone are $5-$7.50. Madras crepes (specialty), served with lentil soup & hot & mild sauces are $3-$4. Pasand has a full bar and live music nightly, no cover charge, minimum 1 beverage per set. ****BEST BUY(5)

KICHIHEI (Japanese), 2084 (Chestnut (Steiner), 929-1670. Dinner includes soup, salad, rice, dessert--a la carte $1 less only)--sashimi & tempura $9.95, sashimi & beef teriyaki $10.15, tempura & chicken teriyaki $9.55, tempura & salmon teriyaki $10.65, pot cookery e.g., shabu-shabu (sliced beef, vegetables cooked in broth & served with dipping sauce) $10.15, seafood, prawns, salmon & vegetables, with dipping sauce $9.15. Good value on Chestnut St. ****BEST BUY(6)

VLASTA'S RESTAURANT (Czech), 2420 Lombard (Scott), 931-7533. 5-11pm except Sun. Entrees served with soup *and* salad. Wiener Schnitzel $9.95, sauerbraten $9.95, 1/2 duck with cabbage and dumplings $9.95, veal roast in champagne $9.95, stuffed cabbage $7.50, goulash $9.50, strudel $1.50, cheese cake $1.50, ice cream $1.25. Good East-European cuisine. ****BEST BUY(6)

GOLDEN DUCK GRILL (Czech), 2953 Baker (Greenwich/Lombard), 922-7144. 1-2:30pm & 5-10pm. Dinner entrees include soup *and* salad--duck with winekraut & dumplings $8.90, veal wienerschnitzel with potato salad $7.95, paprika goulash with dumplings $7.25, paprika chicken $7.25. Marinated herring $2.75, palatschinken (thin crepes Czech-style) $2.95. Small, intimate, picturesque. There's an interesting political story attached to the name--ask. ****BEST BUY(6)

SANPPO (Japanese), 1702 Post (Buchanan), 346-3486. 11:45am-10pm Tue-Sat, 3-10pm Sun. Entrees include soup, pickled cabbage, tea--tempura (shrimp, chicken, fish, vegetables) $5.95 beef with eggplant and ginger $5.95, 8 potstickers $4.50. A favorite. ****BEST BUY(12)

LUPAN'S CAFE (California Nouvelle), 4072 18th St. (Castro), 552-6655. 6-10:30pm Tues-Sun, closed Mon. One of the better restaurants in the Castro area. Appetizers--fettucine in 3-cheese sauce $3.95, fried calamari, both enough for 2, soup with creme fraiche & parmesan $2.50. Entrees--whole red snapper with tomato salsa and French fries $8.25, calves liver $8.50, sweetbreads $11.95, rack of lamb $14.95. Special desserts $3.50. ****BEST BUY(15)

RYAN'S (California Nouvelle), 4230 18th St. (Castro), 621-6131. 6-11pm Mon-Sat, closed Sun. Possibly the best restaurant in the Castro area. Pricewise could also fit in the *Splurge* section. Entrees--BBQ baby back ribs $10, sausages & polenta $9, grilled pork chops $11. ****BEST BUY(15)

CAFE GITANES (Tunesian), 3214 16th St, (Guerrero), 431-5838. 9am-9pm Mon-Thurs, 10am-10pm Fri and Sat, 3-9pmSun. Entrees are served with soup, salad, mint tea--couscous with vegetables $6.95, with chicken $7.45, with fish $8.35, with lamb $9.25; calamari in wine, tomatoes and vegetables $8.35; sausage and lamb stew $8.25; spaghetti with ham, mushrooms, bell pepper, basil and garlic $6.95. Picturesque, elegant setting, large portions. ****BEST BUY(16)

EL TAZUMAL (Salvadoran), 3522 20th St. (Valencia/Mission), 550-0935. 10am-10pm daily. Lunch: $3.95--liver and onions, pork chops, beef tongue in sauce, Spanish omelette, chicken in red sauce. Char-broiled steaks $4.25. House specialty: paella Valenciana $20 for 2. Salvadoran specialties: beef tongue in red wine sauce $5.95; pan-fried whole red snapper $8.50. They also have a taqueria next door which is worth trying. A favorite. ****BEST BUY(16)

RONDALLA (Mexican), 901 Valencia (at 20th St), 647-7474. 11:30am-3am except Mon. Entrees served with guacamole, rice, beans, salad--flautos $5.50; BBQ steak (with tomatoes, onions, potatoes) $6.50; sirloin steak, Mexican style $6.50; pork, Mexican style $6.50. Birria (goat stew) $6.50, fried chicken, Mexican style $6.50. House wine, glass $1.50, fifth $8 (expensive). Nightly entertainment, picturesque. Huge margaritas $1.60. A favorite. ****BEST BUY(16)

MISSION VILLA (Mexican), Mission (20th St) 826-0454. 11am-12pm. Beef soup and vegetables $3.95. Entrees include rice, tortilla, beans, salad, e.g., goat stew $6.75, flautas (tacos with steak, avocado dip and sour cream) $7.25, sliced pork with guacamole $7.25, cactus with pork $6.50, chicken in chocolate sauce $6. Lunch specials 11am-3pm Mon-Fri. $2.95-3.95. One of the oldest Mexican restaurants in the Mission. White tablecloth, cloth napkins. ****BEST BUY(15)

SAN WONG (Szechuan-Mandarin), 1682 Post (Buchanan), 921-1453 and 2239 Clement, 221-1883. 11:30am-10pm daily. Hot and sour soup $2.75, clams with bean-curd $3.25; mongolian beef $4.95, beef with shredded ginger $4.95; steamed, whole fish in wine sauce with ginger $7.95; baby shrimp in hot pepper sauce $6.50, twice cooked pork $4.50, mushu pork $4.50, vegetables deluxe $3.25, egg-plant with garlic sauce $4.50. Very popular, very crowded, very large portions. A favorite. ****BEST BUY(12)(23)

PRINCE NEVILLE'S (Jamaican), 424 Haight (Fillmore/Webster), 861-9433. 5-10 Wed-Sun. Entrees served with soup or salad, rice, peas--saltfish & cabbage $6.95, stewed or curry chickem $5.95, ox-tail $7.95, snapper in wine & vinegar sauce $8.95. Wine $6 liter. ****BEST BUY(14)

HANA (Japanese), 408 Irving (5th/6th Ave.), 665-3952. Lunch 11:30am-2pm Mon-Fri, dinner 5-9pm Mon-Sat. Extremely popular for lunch, so it's best to be early. Lunch details listed under Economical Lunch. Dinner--including soup, salad, pickled cabbage, rice tea--yosenabe (Japanese fish stew with shrimp, oysters, fish, chicken) $6.25, salmon teriyaki $6.95, salmon and sashimi $8.10, and much, much more. A favorite. ****BEST BUY(19)

STOYANOF'S (Greek), 1240 9th Ave (Irving/Lincoln), 664-3664. 10am-9pm except Mon. This restaurant is open for lunch, cafeteria style. Dinners are served with rice pilaf and vegetables. Lamb shish-kebab $8.50; red snapper baked in light sauce of tomatoes, green pepper, lemon, butter and bay leaves $6.50; moussaka (casserole of eggplant baked in layers with lean ground beef and tomato sauce, covered with a bechamel sauce and cheese) $7; spanakopita (chopped spinach and feta cheese baked between layers of filo dough) $6.50; roast leg of lamb $8.50. Appetizers--tarama (fish-egg paste) $2.50, dolma (stuffed grape leaves) $2.50, lemon and rice soup $1.35. ****BEST BUY(19)

AUX DELICES (Vietnamese), 1002 Potrero Ave (22nd ST, opposite S.F. General Hospital), 285-3196. 11am-3pm & 5-10pm Mon-Fri, 5-10pm Sat, closed Sun. Onion soup $1.25 bowl, salad $1.25, pork with mushrooms & bamboo shoots $4.50, sweet-sour shrimp $4.95, chicken with lemon grass $4.95, beef with bean-curd $4.95. Fried banana or ice cream $1. One of best Vietnamese restaurants in the City, bargain prices, a favorite. ****BEST BUY(17)

ASIMAKOPOULUS (Greek), 288 Connecticut (18th St), 552-8789. 11:30am-10pm (dinner from 5pm). Entrees are served with soup or salad--1/2 chicken marinated in lemon and oregano $7.95; lamb stew in wine $8.95; lamb roasted with artichoke hearts and egg-lemon sauce $10.50; filet of snapper sauteed in butter, garlic and olives $8.95. Greek appetizers with hot pita bread $1.95. Large portions but getting pricey. ****BEST BUY(17)

MANDALAY (Burmese), 4348 California (at 6th Ave), 386-3895. 11:30am-3pm and 5-10pm except Mon. Black pepper soup $3.50, deep-fried egg cooked in Burmese sauce $2.75, deep-fried eggplant $3.50, boneless chicken $4.25, beef with garlic and ginger $5.55, large prawns cooked in sauce $6.95. An interesting dessert is a coconut pudding-cake topped with poppyseeds. This cuisine provides new taste sensations, worth a visit. ****BEST BUY(22)

SORENTO (Iranian), 3750 Geary Blvd (Arguello), 751-4530. 4:30-10pm. Persian soup $1.95, cucumber salad $1.45, veal with saffron rice $7.45, ground beef with rice & tomato $5.45, chicken char-broiled $6.45, ice cream $1.25, Persian desserts $1-$2. ****BEST BUY(13)

CINDERELLA BAKERY (Russian), 436 Balboa (5 Av), 751-9690. 9am-6:30pm. Soups (borsht, barley, spinach, kidney) $2.10 bowl, cheese omelette or ham & eggs $2.45. Beef stroganoff, leg lamb with kasha, or cutlet a la Kiev $5.50. Beef, chicken or fish cutlet $4.40. Cabbage rolls or stuffed peppers $4.10, vareniki with cheese $3.80, pirogi $1.60-$1.70. Hearty Russian cooking. Most customers speak the language. A favorite. ****BEST BUY(19)

MAI'S (Vietnamese), 316 Clement (4th Ave), 221-3046 and 1360 9th Ave. (Irving/Judah), 753-6863, 11am-10pm Mon-Sat, 4-9:30pm Sun. Saigon-style soup $3.50. Rice plates: lemon grass BBQ ribs $4.90, lemon grass chicken $4.75, Lalot beef $4.95, coconut chicken $4.75, Vietnamese shabu--fondue with beef, chicken, squid etc. to be cooked do-it-yourself style in chicken broth and soy sauce $8.50; fried prawns, sweet-sour $5.50; sweet-sour fried fish $5.75; spicy pork $4.85. ****BEST BUY(22)(19)

PRESIDIO BAKERY (Russian), Clement & 5th Ave., 752-0393. Wienerschnitzel $4, beef Stroganoff $6.50, pork or polish sausage $4, meatballs with cheese $4, roast lamb $4.50, fried fish & potatoes $4.50. Borsht or spinach soup $1.95, piroshki $1.40. Hearty Russian food without frills, good bakery. ****BEST BUY(22)

TON KIANG (Chinese), 683 Broadway (Stockton), 421-2015 and 5827 Geary (22nd and 23rd Avs), 387-8273 and 3148 Geary (Spruce), 752-4440. 11am-10pm daily. This has expanded into a 3-restaurant chain, specializing in Hakka cuisine of a mountain tribe near Canton. The cooking is different, e.g., the use of wine. A "put-together" meal for 4, consisting of 1 soup and 4 main dishes, can stay within $7-8 per person, e.g., wine-flavored beef soup $4.75, sweet-sour chicken $5.50, mixed vegetables $4, sliced fish in black bean sauce $6, spareribs in orange sauce $5.50, rice 5 portions $2.50. ****BEST BUY(2)(13)

SIAMESE GARDEN RESTAURANT (Thai), 3751 Geary (2nd Av), 668-8763. 5:30-10pm, Tues-Sun. Special dinner $9.95, consists of choice of 2 appetizers and entree, e.g., beef with curry, peanuts, coconut milk; beef with zucchini, hot chili sauce; pork with sweet-sour sauce, onion, pepper. Other dishes--pepper pork sauteed with garlic and pepper $5.95, ginger chicken $4.95, deep fried fish with chili sauce $6.95, beef or pork dishes $4.25-$4.95, chicken and seafood dishes $5.25-$6.95. Elegant Thai dining. A favorite. ****BEST BUY(13)

MAD HATTER, 3848 Geary (3rd Av), 752-3148. 11:30am-9pm MonSat. Bar & restaurant with unusually good food and very reasonable prices. Menu changes often but here are a few examples--rack of lamb $7.95, veal loin $7.25, pot roast $6.25, roast fish with mussels $7.25. ****BEST BUY(13)

ACROPOLIS BAKERY (Russian-Greek), 5217 Geary (6th Ave), 751-9661. 8:30am-9pm daily. Borscht $2.80, Beef Stroganoff $6, stuffed cabbage with sour cream $5, vareniki (ravioli with sour cream) $4.20, dolmades (stuffed vine leaves) $2.80, blintzes $3.20. New ownership but old, longtime cooking staff. BEST BUY****(13)

MARGARITA (Mexican), 19th Ave & Clement, 752-9274. Guacamole with tostaditas $3.75, nachos $5.25. Combination plates with rice, beans & salad--enchilada, chile relleno, tamale, taco (choice of 3) $8.75; enchiladas suiza (filled with cheese, chicken or beef, & covered with green sauce & sour cream dressing) $7.75. Dinner entrees, with rice, beans & salad--2 tamales in husks filled with chicken $7.25, 2 chile rellenos stuffed with cheese & deep-fried $7.25, 2 corn flautas filled with shredded beef, with guacamole & sour cream $7.25. One of best Mexican restaurant outside the Mission. ****BEST BUY(23)

NARAI (Thai-Chinese), 2229 Clement (23 Av) 751-6363. 11am-10pm Tues-Sun. Chow-chow (South China) cuisine, also Thai dishes. Thai egg rolls $3.25, Thai chicken soup in coconut broth & spices $4.75, garlic eggplant $4.95, Thai BBQ chicken with light curry or sweet-sour sauce $5.50, simmered duck in garlic sauce $5.25, pork or beef curry $5.25, prawns with garlic $7.75, squid with garlic & white pepper $5.95, seafood hot pot $10.50, jumbo prawns & silver noodles hot pot $7.75. Extensive lunch menu of soups, rice and noodle dishes $3.25-$3.95. Very interesting cuisine. ****BEST BUY(23)

HAHN'S HIBACHI (Korean), 2121 Clement (21/22 Avs), 221-4246. 11:30am-9:30pm, closed Tues. Dinner includes rice, soup, cucumber salad & sauteed vegetables--(all BBQ items are marinated overnight in special sauce)--pork ribs $7.50, sliced beef $7.50, short ribs $8.25, choice filet $10.95, shrimp or scallops $8.25, grilled fish $6.95, ribeye steak charbroiled $7.50. ****BEST BUY(23)

THE COURTYARD, 2436 Clement (25/26 Avs), 387-7616. 11:30am-2pm and 5-10pm. Dinner entrees served with soup or salad--snapper $7.95, calamari $8.25, 10-oz hamburger $5.95, fettucine Alfredo $7.50, linguini vongole $7.95, 10-oz NY steak sandwich & fries $8.25. This restaurant deserves credit for a first for consumers--they sell wine at retail-shop prices instead of the usual 200-300% restaurant markup. ****BEST BUY(23)

LUNG FUNG (Chinese), 3038 Clement (31/32 Avs), 668-3038. 11:30am-10pm. Sizzling rice soup $3.75, ginger garlic pork $4.75, green pepper beef $4.95, steamed lobster $8.95, pineapple chicken $4.95, 3-seafood & vegetables $5.75, sizzling prawns $5.95, vegetables deluxe $3.95. ****BEST BUY(23)

TSING TAO, (Chinese) 3107 Clement (32nd Ave), 387-2344. 11:30am-9:30pm daily. Szechuan cuisine, some dishes very hot. For 3 or 4 choose among the following: hot and sour soup $2.95, mushi pork (highly recommended) $5.25, pepper prawns $5.95, sizzling beef $5.25, hot braised chicken $4.55, Szechuan eggplant $3.95, shredded pork with garlic. $4.25. Rice 50 cents per portion. An all-time favorite. ****BEST BUY(23)

TOMMY'S (Mexican), 5929 Geary Blvd (23 Av), 387-4747. Yucatan specialties--broiled pork & tomato sauce $6.20, chicken in banana leaves $6.20, garlic shrimp $8.75; marinated rib-eye steak served with rice, beans, guacamole & corn tortillas $8.50. Mexican dishes, served with rice, beans, salad & corn tortillas--chicken, beef or cheese enchilada $4; 2 chile rellenos $6.20, 2 flautas $6.20. Margarita cocktail $1.65, double $3. ****BEST BUY(13)

PINYO (Thai), 4036 Balboa (41/42 Avs), 221-2161. 2 spring rolls $3.25, stuffed chicken wings with pork (specialty) $4.25, charbroiled calamari with spicy sauce $4.50, Thai chicken soup with coconut milk, lemon grass $4.50, prawn salad $5.50. spicy noodles with prawns & bean sprouts $4.95, Panay beef in peanut sauce $4.95, beef with hot pepper, chili, garlic & mushrooms $4.75, snapper with ginger & onion sauce $5.95, ****BEST BUY(23)

MARNEE THAI, 2225 Irving (23/23 Avs), 665-9500. 11am-9:30pm, closed Tues. Imperial rolls (with prawns) $3.25, chicken soup in coconut milk & lemon grass $4.95, silver noodle salad $4.95, ginger chicken $4.95, prawns with hot pepper $6.95. Elegant, one of best Thai rstaurants in the City. A favorite. ****BEST BUY(20)

LA CREMAILLERE (French), 2305 Irving (14 Av), 664-0669. 5-10pm Tues-Sat. Dinner entrees include soup *and* salad--poulet a l'estragon $9.95, sweetbreads $10, lamb chops $11.95. Very pleasant neighborhood restaurant. ****BEST BUY(20)

VERY GOOD***

MARCO POLO (International), 619 Taylor (Post), 775-1028. 12-2pm Mon-Sat, 5-10pm Daily. Dinner entrees served with soup *and* salad, rice, tea--T-bone steak with onions, vegetables, potatoes $8.95 or porterhouse steak $10.95; fried red snapper with black beans or sweet-sour sauce $8.95; grilled pork chops marinated in garlic and spices $6.75; Mongolian prawns sauteed in chili sauce, noodles $8.50; chicken and pork adobo, simmered in spices and served with spicy condiment and rice, $6.75. ***(1)

LITTLE JOE'S (Italian), 523 Broadway (Columbus), 982-7639. 11am-10pm Mon-Sat, Sun 2-10pm. Since moving from Columbus Ave, their lunch prices have jumped but dinner prices are still acceptable, e.g., veal parmigiana $9.75, calves liver and onions $6.75, pot roast $6.75, N.Y.steak $9.25. Soup with meal 75 cents, salad with meal $1.50. ***(3)

GOLDEN KEY (Chinese), 1350 Powell (Broadway), 788-4020. 5-10 Tues-Sat, closed Mon. Won-ton soup $2, Satay beef $4.75, chicken with black mushrooms $4.25, beef with cashew nuts $4.25, 1/2 roast duck $6.25, Kung Pao prawns $5.50, sweet-sour pork $3.75, clay pots $3.75-$5.25. Firepot (Chinese fondue with raw squid, shrimp, beef etc. & broth) for 2 $10. ***(2)

HARRINGTON'S (Irish), 9 Jones (Market/Golden Gate), 431-7441. 11am-3pm daily. Lunch includes soup, vegetables, potatoes, bread and butter. Top sirloin $5.75, liver and onions $3.80, trout $4.25, grilled oysters $4.25, 1/2 lb charbroiled hamburger $4.50, bowl of chili $1.50. Real pub atmosphere. ***(7)

ROONEY'S CAFE (Continental), 1355 Market (9th St), 861-2820. 11:30am-3pm Mon-Fri. Dinner entrees served with soup or salad, e.g., grilled snapper with lime & anchovies, grilled pork loin with rosemary, sage and port-orange sauce $6.95, chicken breast in peanut sauce, avocado & orange slices, chutney $7.50. ***(7)

CARLENE'S (Continental), 1237 Polk (Sutter/Bush), 8am-10:30pm, 441-8200. Dinner entrees served with soup or salad, potato, vegetable & ice cream--e.g., jumbo fried prawns $7.95, scallops $7.45, halibut $7.45. Also, beef stew with salad $5.25, lasagne with soup or salad $6.95, soup & sandwich (11am-3pm) $2.95, soup & salad (all hours) $2.85. ***(10)

WHIRLING DERVISH (Turkish), 1475 Polk (California), 775-7970. Only Turkish restaurant in California. Entrees served with soup or salad and rice pilav--lamb kebab $5.95, Anatolian Rounds (beef & eggs shaped like meat balls and mixed with spiced bread) $4.95. A la carte--mousaka $5.95, tarama (pink caviar) $2.50, humuz (garbanzo-beans mashed with sesame paste), eggplant salad $2.50, yogourt-cucumber-garlic-mint salad $2. ***(10)

BOB'S BROILER, 1601 Polk (Sacramento), 474-6161. Dinners include soup or salad: prawns with tartar sauce $5.95, trout with lemon butter sauce $5.45, grilled red snapper $5.45, halibut steak with mushrooms $6.45, pork chops $4.95, rib-eye steak $5.35. Daily Special: soup & sandwich $2.95. ***(10)

HUNAN COURT (Chinese), 2227 Polk (Green/Vallejo), 928-6688. 11:30am-10pm. Hot & sour soup $2.95, mushu pork (4 pancakes) $5.75, almond chicken $5.50, hunan beef $5.75, sweet-sour prawns $6.50, vegetables deluxe $4.75. A family-dinner for 4 or 5 could stay under $7 each. ***(10)

BEPPLES, 1934 Union (Laguna), 931-6225. 11am-9pm, Sunday from 10am. Express breakfast 6:30-11am. Lunch or dinner pies served with cup soup or coleslaw ($1.25 extra for wine or beer)--chicken pie $5.25, chicken Swiss $5.95, Western (with ground chuck, onions, tomatoes) $4.80, quiche $4.20. Warm muffins with butter $1, dessert pies $1.90-$2.50. Wine 1/2 carafe $2.95, carafe $5.80. Also take-out. ***(5)

COFFEE CANTATA (Continental), 2030 Union (Buchanan), 931-0770. 11:30am-12:30am, later on weekends. Entrees served with soup or salad--e.g., quiche with ratatouille $5.95, pasta with vegetables $5.95, chicken or shrimp curry $7.95, choice of crepes $5.95, seafood pasta $6.95. Soup, salad, quiche $5.95. ***(5)

CAFE MUM'S (Japanese), corner Sutter & Buchanan (Japantown), 931-6986. Lunch (11:30am-4pm) includes soup or salad (seconds)--chicken $4.95, calves liver $5.25, prawns or scallops $5.95, beef curry $4.75. Dinner entrees served with soup or salad (seconds)--filet sole meuniere $7.50, broiled halibut $8.95, prawns or scallops $8.95, fried oysters $6.95, calves liver/onions $6.95, deep-fried pork cutlets $6.95. ***(12)

THE CAFE, 2244 Fillmore (Washington/Clay), 436-9211. 11:30-4pm Mon, 11am-9:30pm Tues-Fri, noon-9:30pm Sat. Entrees served with soup or salad, e.g., moussaka (ground lamb, eggplant and herbs) $3.95, beef Stroganoff $6.25, stuffed shrimp with crab and cheese $6.95, pineapple beef teriyaki $6.50, trout $7. ***(11)

JACKSON FILLMORE (Italian), 2506 Fillmore (Jackson), 346-5288. Cold antipasto (for 1 or 2) $5.25, linguini marinara or pesto $4.50, ravioli $5, tortellini $5.50, linguini with prawns $7.50, prawns a la Jack $9, fried calamari $7.50, eggplant parmigiana $5, veal dishes $9.25. Popular with neighborhood crowd. ***(11)

VIET NAM FRANCE, 1901 Divisadero (Pine), 567-9443. Dinner 5-10pm. Closed Sun-Mon. Dinner entrees served with soup & rice--e.g., chicken or pork with bamboo shoots $4.50, shrimp $5.75, coq au vin $5.75, burgundy beef $6.25, duck in orange sauce $6.75. Also, a number of vegetarian specialities $4.75. Tea 25 cents. ***(11)

KIM'S (Continental, Vietnamese), 508 Presidio Ave. (California), 923-1500. Vietnamese--lemon grass chicken or chicken breast sauteed in lemon grass, and coconut curry sauce and topped with peanuts $4.50; sauteed coconut beef $4.75, sweet-sour prawns & sizzling rice $6.50, calamari & mixed vegetables $4.50, pan-fried fresh catfish or catfish in clay pot $4.95. House special grilled at your table--prawns, sole, scallops, salmon & beef, served with rice noodles and rice paper, fish sauce--$10.50. Continental dishes are a la carte and some are high but par for the area--e.g., shark steak $9.50, English sole $9.50, baked prawns $11.50. Steak is reasonable, e.g., N.Y. steak $8.95, filet mignon $9.50. Chocolate mousse $2, fried banana with ice cream $2. Rice dishes for lunch are plentiful and reasonable, e.g., lemon grass chicken $3.50, lemon grass beef or beef brocolli $3.50, charbroiled lemon grass pork chops $3.75, curry coconut chicken $3.75. ***(11)

CHURCH STREET STATION (American), 2100 Market (14 St, Church), 861-1266. Open 24 hours, daily. Dinner, 4-12 midnight, includes soup or salad, potatoes, vegetable, bread & butter--pan-fried liver with onions & bacon $5.65, charbroiled ground sirloin steak $5.25, charbroiled rib-eye steak $7.95, fish & chips $4.95. Omelettes with home fries, toast & jelly $2.90. Soup $1.15, dinner salad $1.15. Well drinks from the bar 99 cents. ***(15)

JIM'S COUNTRY KITCHEN, 235 Church (Market), 621-3040. 7am-9:30pm. Dinner, with soup or salad & biscuits: pot roast $6.25, center-cut pork chops with apple sauce $5.95, grilled liver with bacon & onions $4.95, fish & chips $5.45. Wine 1/2 l $3, liter $5. ***(15)

SPARKY'S (Italian), 242 Church (Market), 621-8000. Pasta dinners include salad, vegetables, coffee or tea, dessert--cheese ravioli $9.95, fettucine Alfredo $8.95, linguini verde $7.95, spaghetti with Italian red sauce or pesto $6.95. ***(15)

THAI HOUSE, 151 Noe (Henry), 863-0374. 5-10pm. Chicken coconut soup $3.95--can be sensational. Shrimp noodle salad with lemon & chili $4.50, spicy beef with mint leaves or ginger beef $4.95, pork & garlic pepper $4.10, spicy chicken $4.75, chicken green curry $4.95, prawns with silver noodles $7.95, Thai noodles with prawns $3.95. ***(15)

NORSE COVE (Continental) 434 Castro (18th/Market) 626-0462. 7am-10pm. Dinner entrees served with soup or salad, potato, fresh vegetables & French bread--baked meatloaf $5.25, top sirloin steak $7.25, breaded pork chops $6.25, baked lasagne $5.95, beef liver/onions $5.45. 1/2-lb charbroiled burger with fries $4.85. ***(15)

SIAM LOTUS (Thai), 2732 - 24th St (Potrero), 824-6059. Lunch 11:30-2:30pm Mon-Fri, dinner 5-10pm daily. Thai crepes (with shrimp. pork, coconut, peanuts etc.) $4.25, hot pots--lime-prawn soup with lemon grass & mushrooms $5.25. Spicy beef or pork $4.95, lemon grass chicken $4.95, crispy duck $6.25, curry beef or chicken $4.95, lotus ice cream $1.95. ***(15)

RESTAURANT PRADO (Spanish), 3033 24th St. (Harrison),11am-11pm except Wed. Salvadoran and Mexican overtones. Prawn soup $4.95, soup of seven seas $8.75; paella Valenciana $8.95, prawns in wine and garlic $6.95, zarzuela $8.95, liver/onions $4.75, pork chops $4.95. ***(16)

SZECHUAN VILLAGE, 3317 Steiner (Lombard/Chestnut), 567-9989. Hot-sour soup $3.95, sweet-sour pork $5.50, mandarin beef $5.50, sizzling beef platter $6.95, snow-peas shrimps $6.95, honey-chili chicken $6.25, mixed vegetables $5.25. ***(6)

WELCOME MAT (Caribbean), 1341 - 18th St. (Potrero Hill), 647-3663. Lunch 12-2pm Tues-Fri, dinner 6-9:30 Tues-Sat. All entrees served with soup or salad, rice & peas, steamed vegetables. Chicken orange sauce (Trinidad) $6.75, Jamaican curry $6.50, seafood with spices (Martinique) $7, BBQ fish (Barbados) $6.50. Prices somewhat lower for lunch. No MSG or salt. Dishes sound more exotic than they are but the value is good. ***(17)

HARBIN (Chinese-Manchurian), 327 Balboa Street (4th/5th Ave), 387-0274. 11:30-10:30pm daily. Hot-sour soup $2.95, jade fish bowl soup $2.95, moo sue beef with pancakes $5.95, ginger beef $5.55, lichee chicken $5.25, Szechuan shrimp $6.75. ***(19)

EGLANTINE (French), 941 Cole (Frederick), 665-6368. 11am-2:30pm and 6-9:30pm Mon-Fri, Sat and Sun brunch. French country food from the various Provinces. A la carte. Crepe with spinach and camembert, with salad $6.50; trout with champagne or hazelnut sauce $7.95, lamb with garlic and raisin $8.95. Tarte Tatin (apple turnover, enough for 2) $2.95, chocolate or hazelnut mousse $1.95. House wine, 1/2 liter $3.75, liter $5.75. Same dishes at lunch are cheaper. ***(14)

DE WINDMOLEN (Dutch), 120 9th Ave (Irving/Lincoln), 753-0557. 5-9pm. Entrees served with soup or salad--marinated pork on skewers with peanut sauce $6.50, fish of day $5.95, Dutch meatballs with herbs & spices $5.25, 6oz hanburger with fries $2.95, Dutch cheese & fruit $3.50. Only Dutch restaurant in town. ***(19)

LA OLLA, (Mexican-Nicaraguan-Argentinian), 2417 Mission (20th St), 11:30am-9pm Mon-Thurs, Fri and Sat until 10pm. Daily special with salad $4.75. Dinner--charbroiled tortilla specialities--with salad, rice, French fries, tortilla or bread. Nicaraguan steak, in strips $6.95; Argentinian steak (marinated), 12 oz.,$8.95; loin pork $6.50; prawns in sauce $7.25. ***(16)

SPECKMANN'S (German), 1550 Church (27th and 28th St.), 282-6850, 11-2pm Mon-Fri and 12-4pm Sat and Sun, 5-9pm daily. Lunch: bratwurst with potato salad or sauerkraut $4.50, knockwurst with sauerkraut or potato salad $3.95, goulash and spaetzle (Southern German noodles) $5.25. Dinner includes soup (lentil or goulash) or salad--kasseler (smoked pork chop) with sauerkraut and mashed potatoes $8.75; sauerbraten with potato pancakes and red cabbage $9.95, eisbein (pig joint) pickled and boiled $10.75. Typical German Gasthaus fare and ambience. Is becoming pricey. ***(15)

CHEERS (Continental), 127 Clement (Arguello/2 Av), 387-6966. Entrees served with salad--fettucine with salmon $7.95, NY strip steak & vegetables $8.95, grilled trout & vegetables $7.25, mini-calzone with goat cheese $6.75, quiche with ham & mushrooms $5.25. ***(22)

GARDEN HOUSE (Vietnamese), 133 Clement (Arguello/2 Av), 221-3655. 4-10pm. Shrimp & pork rolls $3.75, crab beignets (especially good) $3.75, rice with pork & seafood soup $3.75, lemon-grass chicken $5.45, BBQ pork with rice noodles $5.75, fish in clay pot $5.75. ***(22)

OCEAN (Chinese), 726 Clement (8th Ave), 221-3351, 11:30am-9:30pm daily. Cantonese cuisine. Westlake beef soup (thick with beef, coriander, egg white) $4.50; chicken with onions in clay pot $5.50. Pork Kow Yuk (Hakka-style, bacon steamed several times to reduce the fat) $4.50; saday beef (sauteed beef slices with hot chili and 5-spice) $5; chicken with plum sauce $5. Popular with young Chinese. ***(22)

FOOK (Chinese), 332 Clement (4 Av), 668-8070. Lemon chicken $4.50, chicken with cashew $4.50, spareribs with plum sauce $4.50, curry beef $4.50, spicy prawns $5.75, clay pots $4.50 (e.g., sizzling chicken, beef with green onions, spicy curry beef), mixed vegetables $4.50, crab meat over vegetables $5.50. ***(22)

YUN NAN (Chinese), 832 Clement (9th Ave), 221-2699. 11:30-3pm and 5-10pm except Sun. Hunan and Szechuan cuisine. Lunches--over rice or noodles $3.15-$4.15. Sizzling rice soup $3.15, hot-sour soup $3.15, mushi pork with pancakes $4.95, Szechuan beef $4.95. Yun Nan shrimp $5.95, curry or garlic chicken $4.75, vegetable deluxe $4.75. ***(22)

YET WAH RESTAURANT (Mandarin), 1829 and 2140 Clement (19th and 22nd Avs), 387-8056 and 387-8040. Latter is a lovely garden-like setting. This is a small chain of Mandarin-cuisine restaurants of high quality. Hot and sour soup $3.50, mandarin beef (with scallions sauteed in plum sauce) $6.50, hot and sour pork (with bamboo shoots, onions, peppers) $5.25, ginger fried prawns $6.95, cashew chicken $5.95, noodles with pork and scallions $3.75. ****BEST BUY (23)

EINER'S DANISH, 1901 Clement (20th Ave), 386-9860. 5-10pm daily, to 11pm Fri-Sat, closed Sun. Entrees include soup, e.g., fried petrale sole $8.95, poached trout $7.95, fried oysters $8.95, beef burgundy $7.95. Steak tartar $8.95, Copenhagen beef (ground sirloin) $8.95, Grand Master salad $6.95, German bratwurst, potatoes, vegetables $6.95; cheese fondue for 2 (2 Danish cheeses) $12.95, for 3 $5.50 extra. ***(23)

HAHN'S HIBACHI (Korean), 2121 Clement (22nd/23rd Ave), 221-4246. 11:30am-9:30pm except Tues. Korean BBQ includes soup, rice, cucumber salad, vegetables. All meats seasoned overnight in special sauce--short ribs $8.25, sliced pork $7.50, pork ribs $7.50, shrimp or scallops $8.25, rib-eye steak $7.50. ***(23)

SHENSON'S DELI (Jewish), 5120 Geary (15/16 Avs), 751-4699. 8am-5:45pm Tues-Sun. Lunch plates $4.50--3 potato pancakes &

sour cream, gefillte fish with horse-radish & potatoes, frankfurter & potato salad, chopped liver & potato salad, knockwurst & sauerkraut. 1/2 sandwich with soup or salad $3.50. Sandwich platters with roast kishke or potato pancake, coleslaw--corned beef, pastrami $5.50. Soup with brisket of beef $4.95, with 2 cabbage rolls & kasha $4.95. ***(13)

NEW YORK DELIGHT, 2222 Irving (23/24 Avs), 753-1112. 4-9pm Mon-Sat. Burger & soup or salad, fries $2.95, giant burger $3.85. Entree with soup or salad, potatoes or rice--salmon steak $5.95, broiled sea bass $5.45, N.Y. steak $5.95, roast beef $4.95. ***(20)

ANITA'S KITCHEN (Thai), 1245 Noriega (20th Av), 665-8080. 5-9:30pm except Sun. Includes soup and rice. House curry with prawns $6.95, shrimp and pork brochette $6.95, chicken with herbs and ginger $6.25, deepfried snapper with fresh broccoli and zucchini $6.95, spicy beef or chicken with mint leaves $6.50, Thai combination seafood with lemon grass and herbs $7.95. ***(20)

GOMEN-TEI (Japanese), 5336 Geary Blvd (17/18 Avs), 387-3400. 5pm-2am Tues-Sat, 5-9:30 Sun. Restaurant & sushi bar. Dinner entrees served with soup, salad & rice--sukiyaki beef $6.50, tempura with assorted vegetables & prawns $6.25, with seafood $6.90, yosenabe (soup with seafood, vegetables, bean-cake etc.) $6.50, sashimi $7.95, sushi $6.95-$8.95. Combination dinners--tempura & teriyaki $7.50, tempura & sashimi $7.95. ***(23)

Italian & Basque Dinners

These are among the BEST BUYS of all restaurants in San Francisco. The Italian family dinners are 5-6 course affairs, whereas the Basque dinners are characterized by their *two* entrees (on Friday, meat *and* fish) as well as soup, salad, dessert, and coffee (one includes wine in the price). These are fixed-menu meals, some with a few choices.

Italian Family Dinners

BEST BUY****

CAPP'S CORNER, 1600 Powell (Green), 989-2589, 11:30am-2:30pm & 4-9:30pm. Lunch is $6.25, dinner $10.50, the difference being that lunch has 1 course less (soup *or* salad) and the choice of entrees is more limited than at dinner. N.Y. steak dinner $12.50. A favorite--try the dinner with barley soup & lamb shanks. A favorite. ****BEST BUY(3)

GREEN VALLEY, 510 Green (Columbus/Grant), 788-9384. 11am-2:30pm, 4:30-10pm Tues-Fri 2-10pm, Sat-Sun. Lunch $5.85, dinner $10.35. ****BEST BUY(3)

GOLDEN SPIKE, 527 Columbus (Union/Green), 986-9747. 4-9:45pm Tues-Sun. Antipasto, minestrone soup, salad, pasta, entree, spumoni and coffee $10.95. Entrees include roast beef, chicken cacciatore, veal saute. A big Special every Friday is their crab cioppino, with dinner $11.95. ****BEST BUY(3)

NEW PISA, 550 Green (Columbus/Grant), 362-4726. 2:30-11pm, except Wed. Lunch is $6, dinner $8.50. ****BEST BUY(3)

Other Italian Dinners

i FRATELLI, 1521 Hyde (Pacific/ Jackson), 776-8240. Appetizers--sausage & meat sauce $1.50, garlic bread with olive oil, tomatoes & oregano $2 (more than enough for 2). Pastas--spaghetti bolognese $6.50, with calamari $7.50, with garlic & olive oil $5.50; linguine vongole (with clams) $7.30; tagliatelle (thin fettucine) pesto with basil, garlic, pine nuts & fresh tomatoes $6.75. Canneloni stuffed with ricotta, beef & ham $7.30. Entrees, served with vegetables or pasta--chicken with white wine & mushrooms $7.80, with artichoke hearts & capers $8; veal dishes $11.60-$12.60, fish of day $11. Espresso $1.25, 1/2 liter wine $4.50, liter $8.A favorite. ****BEST BUY(10)

MILANO, 1448 Pacific (Larkin/ Hyde), 673-2961. 5-10pm, except Monday. Gnocchi in gorgonzola cream sauce $8, fettucine with walnut & cream sauce $8, spaghetti with fish or shellfish $8.50, chicken with peppery sauce $8.25, veal scallopps with cheese & lemon butter $9.50, veal chop with rosemary & sage $12.75. Cuisine is exceptional. Appetizers, soups & desserts are somewhat high, pasta and chicken quite reasonable, as is veal, for the quality served. ****BEST BUY(10)

ALLEGRO, 1701 Jones (Broadway), 928-4002. Italian sausage in tomato sauce $3.50 (appetizer), large house salad (for 2) $3. Fettucine Alfredo $6, with pesto $6.50, linguine with sausage $6.75. Chicken cacciatore $8.25, veal scallopini $9.95, seafood fra diavolo

$10, snapper veneziana $9.50. House wine $6.25 carafe. Small, elegant and pleasant. A favorite. ****BEST BUY(Nob Hill).

IRON POT, 441 Washington (Sansome/Battery), 392-2100. 11:30am-2pm and 4:30-10pm, except Sun. Dinner includes minestrone, salad, pasta, ice cream and coffee. Some entrees: roast chicken $8.50, veal milanese $9.50, veal dore $10.25, sole meuniere $9.50. This is an old San Francisco restaurant. ****BEST BUY(8)

PASTA II, 381 S. Van Ness Ave. (15 St), 864-4116. Lunch--minestrone or spinach-mushroom salad $2.50. Pastas--garlic & oil $3.75, Polonaise (with mushrooms, cheese, eggs, parsley) $4, pesto $4.75, vongole $6.75. Dinner--pastas are about $0.75-$1 higher, Alfredo $6.75, with Escargot sauce $8. Chicken tetrazzini (boneless, with mushrooms) $6.75. House wine 1/2 liter $4.25, liter $6.75. ****BEST BUY(16)

CAFE RIGGIO, 4112 Geary Blvd (5/6 Avs), 221-2114. 5-11pm Mon-Sat. Ministrone cup $1.25, bowl $1.95, antipasto $3.95, house salad $2.25. Fettucine Alfredo $6.75, spaghetti al pesto $6.50, stuffed tortellini $6.75, veal parmigiana $8.75, veal piccata $9.75, saltumbocca (veal with ham & cheese) $10.25. Peach melba $1.95, ice cream $1.25, espresso $1.25. Very busy, understandable for the quality and reasonable prices. ***BEST BUY(13)

LA TRAVIATA, 2854 Mission (24/25 Sts), 282-0500. 4-10:30pm, closed Mon. Antipasto (for 2) $5, ministrone $1.25. Lasagne $6, eggplant parmigiana $6.50, other pastas $6.50-$7.50. Veal dishes $11.50-$12, chicken $8-$8.50, sole meuniere $9, calamari $9. Interesting desserts at $2, e.g., cannoli. One of the best Italian restaurants in San Francisco. ****BEST BUY(16)

VERY GOOD***

PASTICI, 561 Columbus (Union/Green), 362-2774. 8am-midnight. Pastas are recommended--sauteed with prawns, spinach, curry & cream $7.75; sauteed with mild Italian sausages, bell-peppers, fresh tomatoes & cream $6.75; with tomato, eggplant & ricotta cheese $7.25. Broiled eggplant wwith soft mozarella cheese, tomatoes, anchovies & oregano $6. Italian mixed salad $2.75, cannoli (a dessert made of pastry shell, ricotta & candied fruit) $1.50. Some appetizers & hot dishes tend to be pricey but above are good value and excellent quality. ***(3)

THE FRONT ROOM, 1500 California (Polk/Larkin), 771-1591. See phonebook for other locations. 11am-midnight (Fri-Sat to 2am). Dinner--including soup, combination salad, garlic bread & ice cream--lasagne $6.95, spaghetti or ravioli with mushrooms & meatballs $6.95, breast of chicken with spaghetti and meat ball $7.25, veal parmigiana or scallopine $8.95. Liter wine $5.25. ***(10)

BUCA GIOVANNI, 800 Greenwich (Columbus), 776-7766. 5:30-11pm Mon-Sat. Ministrone $1.50, fettucine Alfredo $6.65, fettucine with Italian ham $6.85, fettucine with rabbit & chicken sauce $6.95, ravioli with meats, rabbit & chicken sauce $7.95, pasta stuffed with venison $8.25. Veal dishes are $12.95-$18.95, chicken dishes $9.45-$9.85, both on the high side. But lobster tail with Italian sparkling wine relatively cheap at $13.95. The pastas are a great value, large portions. ***(3)

VINCE'S, 5716 Geary Blvd (27/28 Sts), 221-9890. Soup of day cup $1.25, bowl $1.95. Fettucine carbonara or pesto $6.95, linguini with clams $7.95. Dinner entrees--veal with tomato & garlic $9.25, with tomato & cheese $9.75; scallopine marsala $9.25; chicken cacciatore $8.75, with herbs $7.95; sauteed calamari with garlic, tomato & herbs $8.50. Full dinners with soup or salad & pasta $3 additional. ***(13)

GARDEN DINNER HOUSE, 3414 Judah (39th Av), 564-0616. 3:30-8.45pm daily except Tues. Italian dinners include: soup, salad, entree, dessert (ice cream or pie), coffee or tea--chicken cacciatore $6.75, breaded veal cutlet $6.85, veal scallopini $6.95, filet of sole $6.65, fried prawns or scallops, $6.95, sirloin steak $7.50, NY Steak $9.50. ***(20)

PIRRO'S PIZZERIA & RESTAURANT, 2244 Taraval (32nd Av), 731-4545. 4:30-11:30pm daily. Dinner includes soup, salad, coffee, dessert--spaghetti $7.25, ravioli $7.50, spaghetti and meatballs $8., lasagna $8.10. Special dinner for 2--lasagna and canneloni, 1/2 liter wine, soup, salad, coffee, dessert $17.50. ***(20)

DI GRANDE, 1439 Taraval (39 Av), 665-0325. 4:30-9:30pm. 6-course family-dinner $10.95. Choice of entree, e.g., stuffed pepper, eggplant parmigiana, filet sole. ***(20)

Basque Dinners

BEST BUY****

OBRERO HOTEL, 1208 Stockton (Pacific, 986-9850. A 7-course dinner ($9.50) starts at 6:30pm sharp, includes soup, salad, *two* entrees, dessert, wine, and coffee. Examples are (Monday) oxtail stew and roast beef; (Wednesday) clams with pasta and roast pork; (Friday) rex sole and lamb. Family atmosphere, a favorite. ****BEST BUY(2)

DES ALPES, 732 Broadway (Stockton/Powell), 788-9900. 5:30-10pm $8.50. Fri. $9.00. Menu is different each day and posted for the week, e.g., Wed beef tongue with mushrooms & choice of roast lamb or fish, Fri trout or steamed clams & filet of beef, Sat lamb stew or filet sole and roastbeef. French-Basque. ****BEST BUY (3)

THE BASQUE HOTEL, 15 Romolo Place (near Broadway/Columbus), 788-9404. 5:30-9:30pm Tues-Sun. $8.50 Tues-Thurs and $9 Fri-Sun. Dinner includes *two* entrees, soup, dessert, coffee. Owner is Spanish-Basque. ****BEST BUY(3)

VERY GOOD

CAFE DU NORD, 2170 Market (Church), 626-0977. 5:30-9:30pm Wed-Sun. $11.95. Meal consists of soup, hors d'oeuvres, *two* entrees, salad, dessert (creme caramel), coffee. Friday dinner is $13.25 and includes clams and filet mignon. Pricier than the other Basque restaurants. ***(3)

Early Dinners

A number of restaurants have begun to offer "Early Dinners" at $6.95 and $7.95, some a bit higher, between 4 and 7pm. Most are for weekdays only. A few are valid weekends, too. These dinners include soup or salad, entree and, a few, drink or dessert. Most are seafood restaurants, some among my favorites in the city. The obvious reason for these wonderful offers is: competition. Of course, you have to be there early but it's worth the effort. Most of these restaurants are white-tablecloth, cloth-napkin, flowerson-the-table kind. In other words, elegant. Take advantage of the offer! Since some of these restaurants may discontinue their specials for the tourist season, be sure to check first.

BEST BUY****

THE SQUARE in Chancellor Hotel, 433 Powell (Union Square), 362-2004. 5-7:30pm Mon-Fri. $8.95, includes soup or salad, beverage, ice cream and entree, e.g., grilled veal chops with pasta, filet sole, canneloni, ravioli. ****(BEST BUY(1)

MAYES, 1233 Polk (Sutter/Bush) 474-7674. 3-6pm Mon-Fri. $8.25. Includes soup, salad, choice of 4 entrees. Same dinner for Seniors is $7.25. ****BEST BUY(10)

PISCES SEAFOOD, 2127 Polk (Broadway/Vallejo), 771-0850. 5-6:30pm, 4-5:30pm Sun $6.25-$6.75, including clam chowder or salad, entrees, e.g., petrale sole, red snapper, trout, calamari. ****BEST BUY(10)

AKASAKA (Japanese), 1721 Buchanan (Japan Center). 5:30-7pm Mon-Fri. $7.95, includes soup, salad, rice, tea and choice of tempura, chicken teriyaki, sushi & tempura and assorted sushi. ***BEST BUY(12)

CAESAR'S (Italian), corner Bay & Powell, 989-6000. 4:30-6pm Tues-Fri. $7.95, includes salad, soup, entree & coffee. Choice of chicken, baked ham, pot roast, ground sirloin steak, filet sole. Also, Senior's Special. ****BEST BUY(4)

MITSUKO'S (Japanese), 2120 Greenwich (Fillmore), 563-9409, 5:30-11pm, closed Sun. Sunset Dinner Special 5:30-7:30pm $6.95, includes soup, salad, pickle, sake or wine, tempura & chicken teriyaki. ****BEST BUY(6)

MARINA CAFE, Scott (Lombard), 929-7241. 5-7pm (Sat-Sun 4-6pm).$7.95. Includes soup or salad and choice of 7 entrees, e.g., snapper, coho salmon, calamari, pasta of the day. Fish is mesquite-broiled. ****BEST BUY(6)

GRAND VICTORIA (French), 1607 Haight (Clayton), 861-4346. 5:30-6:30pm. $7.95. Includes soup or salad and choice of 4 entrees, e.g., roast leg of lamb, roast duckling. ****BEST BUY(14)

LUCKY FRENCH PIERRE BISTRO, 200 23rd Ave (California), 386-3571. $5.95. ****BEST BUY(23)

SOUTH PACIFIC (Polynesian), 2500 Noriega (32nd Av) 564-3363. 5-6pm daily, Sun 4-6pm. Includes clam chowder or salad, coconut ice cream and choice of entree, e.g., shrimp louie, snapper, sole, trout. ****BEST BUY(23)

IL GIARDINO (Italian), 215 West Portal, 566-5700. $7.95, complete dinner. ****BEST BUY(21)

PIERRE'S D'ANJOU, 2325 Taraval (33/34 Avs), 564-4464. 4:30-6pm, Tues-Fri. $7.50. Soup or salad, ice cream or sherbet, coffee or tea & choice of entree e.g., red snapper, sole with champagne sauce, veal stew with mushrooms. ****BEST BUY(20)

VERY GOOD***

YAMATO (Japanese), 717 California (Grant Av), 397-3456. 5-6:30pm, Mon-Fri. $10.50. Choice of sukiyaki prepared at table, sesame chicken, NY steak, broiled chicken or sushi, together with catch of day. ***(2)

SAN FRANCISCO MARRIOT, Fisherman's Wharf, Bay & Columbus Ave., 775-7555. 5-7pm. $8.45. Complete dinner, choice of prime rib, chicken piccata, red snapper or seafood pasta. ***(4)

SILVER CLOUD, 1994 Lombard (corner Webster), 922-1977, 5-7pm. Complete dinner--which includes soup or salad, ice cream or cheese cake, coffee and glass of pinot chardonnay--for price of entree only, e.g.,sauteed prawns $10.95, lobster tail $13.95, veal scallopini $13.95, seafood combination $9.95, crab louis $9.95. Another special is 6 oysters $2.95. ***(6)

DISH, corner Masonic & Haight, 431-3534. 6-7:30pm Mon-Fri, 4-6pm Sat-Sun. $4.95-$5.95--Includes soup or salad and choice of entree--prawn fettucine, grilled pork chops, teriyaki chicken, grilled mahimahi. ***(14)

SUNSET JOE'S, 1358 9th Ave, 759-8090. $5.95. ***(19)

MAI'S (Vietnamese), locations on Clement, 9th Av & Union Sts, see phonebook for exact locations and phone numbers. Dinner Special $5.95. Includes soup, appetizer, main dish, rice and tea. ***

GOOD TOKYO (Japanese), 546 Clement (5th Av), 367-6688. 5-7pm $7.95. Includes soup, salad, rice, dessert, and sashimi or beef or chicken teriyaki. ***(22)

BLUE POINT, 951 Clement (11th Av), 752-5927. 4-7pm $7.95. Includes soup or salad, glass of wine and entree, e.g., seafood platter, trout, snapper, sole, 1/2 broiled chicken. ***(22)

FISHERMAN'S CAFE, 7001 Geary (34 Av), 751-0191. 4-6:30pm. $7.95. Includes soup or salad, coffee or tea, ice cream, entree, e.g., red snapper, seafood, sole Monterey. ***(13)

CAPTAIN'S SCOTT GROTTO, 3028 Taraval (40th Av), 665-4038, 5-7pm $5.95. Includes soup or salad and entree, e.g., calamari, fried prawns, snapper, sole dore (N.Y. steak $7.50). ***(20)

Fish Restaurants & Oyster Bars

San Francisco is famous for its seafood. I've omitted the more expensive fish restaurants and have concentrated on those that give value as well as high quality. I've also included Oyster Bars in this section because they serve some of the best seafood in San Francisco.

There are a few counter-style very simple oyster bars in the City that provide very good fish-eating, especially salads, cocktails, oyster and clams. A few, with a few more elegant ones thrown in for good measure, will be found at the end of this chapter. They do not carry star ratings. I consider them all ****BEST BUY.

Most Chinese restaurants include fish dishes, some specialize in fish. An especially good Chinese restaurant for crab, whole fish etc., is Yuet Lee (1300 Stockton, corner Broadway, 982-6020). But most other Chinese restaurants with 3-4 stars will also have good fish dishes.

BEST BUY****

Seafood Restaurants

JADE GARDEN SEAFOOD RESTAURANT, 674 Broadway (Grant/Stockton), 956-4027. 11am:10:30pm, closed Tues. $23 seafood dinner for 4--seafood soup, steamed oysters in half-shell, sauteed chicken & shrimp, king clams & brocolli, pan-fried sand dab, steamed rice, tea. $48 dinner for 6--dried scallop soup, steamed oysters in half-shell, chicken & shrimp basket, king clams with broccoli, whole lobster or crab, whole steamed fish, fried rice, tea. Many single dishes from $4.50 (e.g., squid with shrimp sauce) to $6 (e.g., seafood basket of shrimps, scallops, rock cod, squid). Also a full menu of pork, beef and chicken dishes at reasonable prices. ****(2)

MAYES OYSTER HOUSE, 1233 Polk (Sutter/Bush), 474-7674. Over 100 years old. Recently under new management with an aggressive program, including Early Dinner, Senior Specials, etc. Snapper $7.95, sand dabs $7.95, sea bass $8.95, swordfish $9.90, fettucine Alfredo $6.50, veal scallopine with mushrooms and marsala $8.25, broiled lobster $12.95. For $4.50 more you can have a colossal dinner including soup, shrimp cocktail, pasta, ice cream or cheese, tea or coffee. A good deal if you're hungry. ****BEST BUY(10)

ADRIATIC, 1755 Polk (Clay), 771-4035. 11:30-2:30pm, 5:30-10pm. Seafood platter $8.25, filet of snapper $7.50, filet of bass (recommended) $8.95, fish stew $7.95, frog legs $8.95, green salad $1.50, soup $1.50. Also beef, lamb, veal, poultry dishes at comparable prices. House wine is also good, 1/2 liter $3.50, liter $6.50. As you know, I don't normally like a la carte restaurants--unless they are reasonably-priced and have very good food--such as this one. A favorite. ****BEST BUY(10)

PISCES, 2127 Polk (Broadway/Vallejo), 771-0850. Lunch 11am-3pm, Mon-Sat, dinner 5-10:45pm Mon-Sat, 4-10pm Sun. Dinner with clam chowder or salad, vegetables and fries or rice and entree, e.g., calamari steak $7.95. Combination $7.95, trout $7.50, halibut $6.95, sea bass $8.75. Complimentary glass of wine. Small, elegant. A favorite. ****BEST BUY(10)

LA ROCA (Mexican), 4288 24th (Castro), 282-2870. Entrees served with black beans, rice or vegetables--red snapper with garlic sauce $8.50, scallops with squid & oysters $9.50, paella $11.25, bouillabaisse $9.95, steamed clams in garlic sauce $8. Wine 1/2 liter $3.50, liter $6. ****BEST BUY(15)

TON KIANG (Chinese), 683 Broadway (Stockton), 421-2015 or 5827 Geary (22nd & 23rd Avs), 387-8273. 11am-10pm Mon-Sat. 7-Course family fish dinner for 5-6 persons $45. Includes a whole crab and whole fish. It also includes the traditional chicken feet as one course; if you prefer, they will substitute for another dish e.g., barbecued ribs (delicate). This meal does not appear on the English menu, so ask for it. Very good feast meal. Also Hakka dinner for 5-6 with chicken, beef, spareribs, whole crab, whole fish $45. Recommended for "big occasions". ****BEST BUY(3)(13)

RED CRANE (Chinese), 115 Clement, (12th Av), 751-7226, 11:30am-10pm. This is a Chinese seafood and vegetable restaurant. Soups: seafood $5.50, vegetarian hot-sour $3. Snow peas & prawns $5, ginger garlic squid $4.25, sliced fish with black bean sauce $4.25, sweet-sour walnuts $4.75, black mushrooms with vegetables $4.50, scallops Hunan $5.75, steamed whole fish $10, vegetable chow mein $3.95, chow mein with 3 kinds of mushroom $3.25. BEST BUY(22)

SILVER MOON (Chinese), 2301 Clement (24 Av), 386-7852. 11:30am-10pm. Can make excellent family dinner of fish or vegetarian dishes. Crab meat soup $3.75, vegetarian hot-sour soup $3.25, sizzling prawns $5.50, vegetarian duck or chicken (and looks like it!) $4.25, sliced fish with black bean sauce $4.50, Szechuan eggplant $3.75, abalone with black mushrooms $5. ****BEST BUY(23)

SUNSET PIER, 3044 Taraval (40 Av), 665-5648. Entrees served with soup *and* salad, French bread & rice, e.g., steamed clams in wine & butter-garlic sauce $6.75, filet sole $5.95, calamari saute in wine & garlic-butter $6.75, breaded scallops $7.50, stuffed sole (with crab, shrimp etc.) $8.50, crab cioppino $8.50. ****BEST BUY(20)

VERY GOOD***

GOLDEN KEY (Chinese), 1350 Powell (Broadway), 788-4020. 5-10pm, closed Mon. Seafood dinner for 5-6 $42--seafood soup, steamed eel with black bean sauce, prawns, clams in black bean sauce, stuffed fish (with shrimp etc.), oysters & broccoli, whole live crab, tea. Also, a $25 seafood dinner for 3-4 or a $16-$18 lobster dinner for 2. ***(2)

ERNIE'S NEPTUNE FISH GROTTO, 1816 Irving (19th Ave), 566-3344, 11am-3pm and 5-10pm Tues-Sat. Lunch, with clam chowder or salad, $5, e.g.,rex sole, sand dabs. Dinner entrees served with shrimp c ocktail, clam chowder, ice cream and coffee, e.g., brook trout $8.25, halibut $9.25, red snapper $9.05. This a businesslike, old seafood restaurant. ***(20)

RIVERSIDE (Chinese), 3614 Balboa (38 Av), 221-2211. 11am-9pm. Seafood dinner for 4-5 $35--seafood soup, mixed seafood in nest, clams with black bean sauce, prawns with greens, whole crab with ginger & garlic sauce, whole steamed fish. Also, non-fish menu, e.g., hot-sour soup $3.60, cashew chicken $4.25, beef & greens $4.50, prawns with cashews $6.25. ***(20)

CAPTAIN SCOTT'S GROTTO, 3028 Taraval (4oth Av), 665-4038.5-9:30 pm except Sun. Dinner includes clam chowder or salad, coffee and dessert--e.g., swordfish, salmon, crab cioppino $7.95. Daily specials with soup or salad $5.95-6.95, e.g., halibut, bouillabaisse. ***(20)

Oyster bars

RANDY'S OYSTER BAR, at Lehr's Greenhouse, 750 Sutter, 474-6464. 6:30am-9:30pm. (1)

SWAN OYSTER DEPOT, 1517 Polk (California/Sacramento), 673-2757. No-nonsense, counter-only eating place. Cocktails--shrimp $3.75, prawns $3.95, crab $4.75, lobster $5.95. Salads--shrimp $7.50, prawns $8.75, crab $9.95, lobster $11.75. Eastern oysters (6) $3.25, clams $3.25. Clam chowder cup $1.50, bowl $2.75. Always crowded.(10)

RAW BAR RESTAURANT, 1509 Hyde (Jackson/Pacific), 928-9148. Caesar salad $2.95, prawn cocktail $3.95, hot lobster tail salad $4.95, oysters (6) $4.95. With vegetables, baked potato or pilaff rice--sea bass $8.95, swordfish steak $7.95, halibut $7.95, lobster tail $8.95, steamed mussels $7.95, steamed clams $8.95. (1)

LaROCCA'S OYSTER BAR, 3519 (California (Laurel), 387-4100.(11)

P.J.'S OYSTER BED, 2299 Van Ness Ave, 885-1155 & 737 Irving, 566-7775. (11)(19)

ANCHOR OYSTER, 579 Castro (19 St), 431-3990. Cocktails--Shrimp $3.95, crab or prawn or combination $4.95. Oysters (6) $4.95, clams $3.95. 1/2 cracked crab, salad, bread & butter $8.95. Boston clam chowder cup $1.95, bowl $2.95. 12 oysters, 8 clams, 4 prawns, bread & butter $16.95, 1/2 order $8.95. (15)

BANGKOK EXPRESS, 907 Irving (10 Av), 731-0670. 6 bluepoint (oysters $3.95, 6 cherrystone clams $3.95, clam chowder cup $1.10, bowl $2.50. Dinners, with soup or salad, vegetable, potatoes or rice, mesquite-broiled, snapper, $5.95 trout $6.25, mahi-mahi $6.50 etc. (19)

Steak

BEST BUY****

ORIGINAL JOE'S, 144 Taylor (Market), 775-4877. 10:30am-1.30am. In Splurge range. Top sirloin (14oz) $10.50, N.Y. cut (14oz) $11.50, (18oz) $13.95, filet mignon (18 oz) $16.75. All come with ravioli or spaghetti and vegetables or French fries. Also, a wide range of Italian foods. ****BEST BUY(1)

POLO'S, 34 Mason (Market), 362-7719, 11am-11pm Mon-Sat. One of the oldest Italian restaurants in the city. Their charbroiled steaks--after 5pm--are a specialty and are served with spaghetti, ravioli or vegetables, e.g., N.Y. cut, 12-14 oz, $10.25; rib 16 oz, $10.25; top sirloin, 16 oz, $9.75; veal T-bone 14 oz $10.25; French lamb chop $9.50. ****BEST BUY(9)

THE MAGIC GRILL, formerly Butcher Block (Vietnamese), 2348 Polk (Union), 771-5544, 5:30pm-10:30pm daily. Includes soup or salad. N.Y. steak (12oz) $11.95, filet mignon (10oz) $12.95, entre-cote with pepper $7.85, steak Dianne $8.50. ****BEST BUY(10)

VERY GOOD***

GEARY STEAK HOUSE (cafeteria), 901 Geary (Larkin), 776-6300. 11am-11pm. Charbroiled N.Y. steak (12oz) $5.30, club (12oz) $6.30, filet mignon (10oz) $7. Includes green salad, baked potato, garlic roll. ***(9)

NAPOLITANA PIZZA (Italian), 180 Church St. (Market), 552-9490. 11:30am-11pm, Fri-Sat to 1am, Sun 4-11pm. 16-oz steak & mush-rooms $9.45. 18" pizza $7.75-$8.30, spaghetti or ravioli with meat-balls, soup & salad $6.45. ***(15)

CAPRI PIZZA (Italian), 2272 Market (16 St), 552-3000). 16-oz steak with spaghetti $9.85. Spaghetti with meatballs, soup & salad $6.45. ***(15)

PALACE STEAK HOUSE, 3047 Mission (Army), 647-2011. 11am-11pm Mon-Sat, 1-10pm Sun. One hour courtesy parking. With green salad, bread & baked potato--N.Y. cut (12 oz) $5.25, club (14 oz) $6.25. Charbroiled. ***(16)

BULLSHEAD, 3745 Geary (Arguello/ 2nd Av), 668-2323 and 840 Ulloa (West Portal) 665-4350. Noon-10pm. All steaks come with soup or salad bar (repeats), potatoes or rice, vegetables and French bread. T-bone 16oz $12.95; N.Y. steak 10 oz $10.95, filet mignon 8oz $10.95, 12 oz $12.95. ***(13)(21)

951 CLEMENT, 951 Clement (12 Av), 387-4033. Dinner entrees include soup or salad, vegetables, potatoes or rice--12oz NY cut $11.50, filet mignon, 2 pieces, $12.95, 12oz ground sirloin with fruit & shoestring potatoes $6.95. Elegant setting. ****BEST BUY(22)

Ribs

BEST BUY****

SIZZLER, 398 Eddy (Leavenworth), 775-1393. See under Salad Bars. Their ribs are always a good buy, especially when they have the all-you-can-eat Special for $7.99. ***(9)

VICTORIA STATION, Embarcadero (Broadway), 433-4400. 11:30am-2pm & 5:30-10pm. 3-ribs & salad bar (all-you-can-eat) $6.95 at lunch, $8.75 at dinner. All-you-can-eat ribs & salad bar (all-you-can-eat) $9.95 at lunch or dinner. ****BEST BUY(8)

CLOWN ALLEY, 2499 Lombard (Divisadero), 931-5890. Fri-Sat only. BBQ ribs with salad & bread $5.50. Restaurant is open 24 hours a day, 7 days a week. ****BEST BUY(6)

SAN FRANCISCO BBQ (Thai), 1328 18th St. (Missouri/Texas), 431-8956. 11am-2pm and 4:30-9:30pm Tues-Sun. Specialty is BBQ pork ribs (with spices, garlic) $4.85. Other BBQ items: 1/2 chicken

$3.50, squid salad $3.25, lamb $5.75, frog legs $6.20. Bowl beef noodle soup $4, practically a beef stew. ****BEST BUY(20)

FIREHOUSE N0.1, 501 Clement (5th Av), 386-5882. 11:30am-10pm. 1/2 cut pork or beef ribs $4.50, full cut $7.95. Sampler for two $7.95--ribs, chicken, links--$13.95, baby-back ribs 1/2 rack $6.25, rack $11.90. Eat-in, take-out. No-nonsense rib-eating. A favorite. ****BEST BUY(22)

VERY GOOD***

NICKIE'S BBQ, 460 Haight (Fillmore), 621-0249. With potato salad, baked beans, corn bread--spareribs $7, 1/2 BBQ chicken $5.95, beef & BBQ $6.95. T-bone steak with baked potato, vegetable, salad, bread $7.95. ***(14)

A DELI LOVER'S CAFE, 442 Haight (Fillmore), 626-1523. 7am-10pm. Daily Specials include salad, corn bread & 2 side dishes--pork chops $5.95, meat loaf $4.95, sirloin steak $5.95, fish $4.95, BBQ beef rib $6.50. Fish and BBQ beef ribs Thurs-Sun. ***(14)

LEON'S BARBEQUE, 1913 Fillmore (Pine), 922-2436 and 2800 Sloat Blvd. (46th Av), 681-3071. 11am-10pm. LEON'S CAJUN & CREOLE CUISINE, 3800 Taraval (46 Av), 759-1523 also belongs to this group. Lunch or dinner plates include corn muffin and choice of baked beans, potato salad, spaghetti or coleslaw. Lunch--pork or beef ribs $4.95, 1/2 chicken or hot links $4.50. Dinner--pork or beef ribs $8.25, 1/2 chicken $4.75, hot links $6.25. Sampler $8.50. ***(11)(23)

HOME STYLE BBQ, 600 5th Ave. (Balboa Av), 668-9388. 8am-9pm Mon-Fri, 10am-10pm Sat, closed Sun. Hawaiian-style BBQ. With baked beans, roll, butter--spareribs or beef ribs $4.05, combination $4.25, hot links $3.50, 1/2 chicken $3.50. Sweet-sour spareribs $3.50, sandwiches with salad & fries--BBQ beef $3.45, 6-oz hamburger & fries $2.75. Large portions $7.25, combination $7.50. ***(19)

COLLIER'S BBQ, 1516 Ocean (Miramar), 585-6568. 4:30-12pm Mon-Thur, Fri & Sat 11am-2:30pm, Sun 12-9pm. Spareribs with choice of coleslaw or beans $7.50, links $4.95, ribs and links $9.95, slab of ribs for 3 or 4 $15.50. Also BBQ fish. Sweet potato pie $1.25. ***(20)

BIG HORN BBQ, 808 Geary (Hyde), 776-5619. 12 noon to mid-night. Pork spareribs with baked potato or fries and hot French bread $6.15; also with soup, salad, coffee or tea $7.65. BBQ chicken $4.75 & $6.25, respectively. ***(10)

Natural Food & Vegetarian

San Francisco has a large number of vegetarian restaurants, some of gourmet quality, so if you are a vegetarian you'll have no trouble eating here. A tip for vegetarians: join the S.F. Vegetarian Society, 1450 Broadway, San Francisco, CA 94109 (phone 775-6874 or 776-3960). This group has a comprehensive list of restaurants and salad bars that give their members a discount. Membership $12/year.

BEST BUY****

LOTUS GARDEN (Chinese), 532 Grant Ave (California), 397-0707. Closed Mon. Hot-sour soup $3.25, spring roll $2.45, deluxe mixed vegetables with noodles $3.85, straw mushrooms with vegetables $4.35, 2 kinds mushrooms with broccoli $5.25, stuffed eggplant $5.25, combination vegetarian $4.25, hot walnut pudding $1.50. Elegant. ****BEST BUY(2)

TURNING EARTH RESTAURANT, 13 Columbus Av (Pacific), 391-6307, 11:30am-2:30pm Mon-Sat. A collective dedicated to ecology. They serve 4-6 salads which change daily, 1 salad $2, 2 salads $3, 3 salads $4. They also serve 2 homemade soups daily, e.g., enchilada or garden chili $2.50. Also a number of sandwiches $3-$3.50. Coffee, tea 50 cents, apple juice or hibiscus tea punch 75 cents, fresh-squeezed orange juice $1.25. ****BEST BUY(2)

AMAZING GRACE, 216 Church (17 St), 626-6411. Cafeteria. 11am-10pm Mon-Sat. Entree with vegetables & brown rice $4.60, with cup of soup $5.16. Sandwich with cup soup $3.76. Salad bar $3.59/lb (expensive). Casserole dish, e.g., spinach lasagna $4.25, shepherd's pie $3.10. Curry, e.g., mushroom $3.10, soups $1.15 cup, $2.15 bowl. ****BEST BUY(15)

GOVINDA'S (formerly 7-Mothers), 86 Carl (Cole), 753-9703. Full meal consisting of soup, bread, salad, entree & dessert $6. ****BEST BUY(14)

THE HIGHER TASTE AYURVEDA (Indian), 775 Frederick (Arguello), 661-7290. Hare Krishna. Lunch 11:30am-2pm Mon-Sat., dinner 5-8pm Mon-Sat. Near UC Medical Center. 5-course lunch--vegetables, soup & salad $3.75; 7-course dinner with soup & salad $5. Menu changes daily, also have curry and tempura dishes, homemade chutneys, savories and sweets. ****BEST BUY(19)

HARVEST MOON, 339 Judah (8th/9th Av), 664-3044, 1oam-9pm. Omelettes with 3 eggs, 9-grain bread $1.95; with cheese, avocado, sour cream, each item additional 40 cents. 2 eggs, home fries, 9-grain toast $2.65. Large green salad with sprouts and tomatoes $2.75. Raw vegetable salad $2.75, fruit salad with yogurt $2.75, bowl of soup with 9-grain bread $1.95. Dinner--including soup and salad, tea or coffee--lasagna $5.50, vegetable family dinner $5.40. Cheese-yogurt pie (specialty) $1.50. Simple, clean, lunchroom style. ****BEST BUY(19)

RED CRANE (Chinese), 1115 Clement (12 Av), 751-7226. See under Fish Restaurants. A favorite. ****BEST BUY(22)

SILVER MOON (Chinese), 2301 Clement (21 Av), 386-7852. See under Fish Restaurants. A favorite. ****BEST BUY(23)

VEGI-FOOD (Chinese), 1820 Clement (19th Av), 387-8111. 11:30am-3pm and 5-9pm Tues-Fri, no break on Sat-Sun. Hot and sour soup $3.25, 8 vegetables $3.55, walnuts sweet & sour $4.50, vegetable deluxe (with 4 kinds of mushrooms, 2 kinds of fungus, tofu, gluten), an absolute favorite, $5.95, braised bean curd with black mushrooms and greens $4.50. Top Chinese quality, elegant decor, No MSG. ****BEST BUY(23)

VERY GOOD***

SUNSHINE JUICE BAR & RESTAURANT, 1718 Polk (Clay), 441-3313, open 11am-9pm daily. Mostly lunch-type items,e.g.,soups, juices, sandwiches juices. 1/2 egg or humus sandwich and soup (cup) $2.50, with bowl of soup $3.25. Soup and salad $3. Evening specialties daily, e.g., ratatouille (vegetable stew), salad, bread and butter $3.75. ***(10)

CHESTNUT CAFE, 2016 Fillmore (Pine), 922-6510, 9am-5pm Mon-Sat. Breakfast: 2 eggs, toast, butter, coffee $1.80; sandwich and soup $2.95, small salad and soup $2.45, soup $1.25. ***(11)

REAL GOOD KARMA, 501 Dolores (18th St), 621-4112. 11:30am-2:30pm, and 5-10pm Mon-Fri, 5-10pm Sat-Sun. Daily lunch special with soup and salad $3.95, e.g., tempura with 5 vegetables and tofu, with soup and salad $6.75; mushroom fried rice and vegetables $4.35. Ice cream (made with honey) $1.35. ***(15)

DIAMOND STREET RESTAURANT, 737 Diamond (24th St), 285-6988. 5:30-10pm daily. Pasta with pesto $6.25, calamari almandine $7.95, spinach and walnut lasagna $5.95, broiled salmon or swordfish $9.50 (in season). Desserts are high ($2.50). Live classical guitar Sundays. A bit pricey but good-quality international cuisine.***(16)

CAFE SANTE (formerly Hungry Mouth), 11 Clement (Arguello), 386-9792.***(22)

The following vegetarian restaurants are also recommended:

PASAND MADRAS CUISINE (Indian), 1875 Union (Laguna), 922-4498. (5)

THE CHAC CAFE, 3870 17th St, 861-1878. (15)

PHAI HA, 1125 Clement, 752-0888. Asian vegi. (22)

GANGES, 775 Frederick, 661-7290. (14

ANANDA-FUARA, the Sri Chin Moy Restaurant, 3050 Taraval, 564-6766. (20)

SHANGRI LA, 2026 Irving, 731-2548. Chinese veg

VII. Splurge Restaurants, $10-$15 Per Person

BEST BUY****

JANOT'S (French), 44 Compton Place (behind Gump's), 392-5373.
11:30am-10pm. San Francisco's newest French "find". Appetizers
are high but good, e.g., warm duck confit $7.50, warm spinach & ba-
con salad--all done innovatively and quite enough for 2 as appetizer.
Entrees--lamb chops with French beans & noodles $15, NY steak
with fries & French beans $13, fish specials in butter sauce $11.
Desserts are also innovative, $3-$4. Well worth the money.
****BEST BUY(1)

LE CENTRAL (French), 453 Bush (Grant/ Kearny), 391-2289. San
Francisco's closest to a reasonably-priced good French brasserie.
Cold cuts $10.50, beef bourgignon $9.95, cassoulet $9.95, choucroute
Alsatian $10.50, rack of lamb $15.50, filet salmon $13.45, steak &
fries $15.25. Espresso $1.75. ****BEST BUY(8)

LAFAYETTE (French), 290 Pacific (Battery),986-3360. 11am-
10:30pm. Recommended for dinner only. Artichoke soup with hazel-
nuts & cognac $2.95, green salad with baby shrimps, confit of duck
salad with walnut oil $5.50. Entrees--Sonoma sausages with baked
lentils $8.95, breast of chicken with raisins & almond sauce $9.95,
legs of duck simmered in Cabernet Sauvignon $9.95, steamed fresh
sea bass in white wine & cream $11.95, rack of lamb $15.95. Desserts $3.25-$3.75. Reasonably-priced for the quality of French cooking. ****BEST BUY(8)

LA BERGERIE (French), 4221 Geary (6th/7th Av), 387-3573, 5-
10pm Tues-Sat. Includes soup, salad, ice cream, coffee. Civet de
lapin (rabbit braised in red wine, herbs, juniper berries and saupiquet
sauce) $12.50, filet of sole stuffed with shrimp and baked in parch-
ment $11.50, coq au vin $11, whole broiled Maine lobster $17.50.

Prices have gone up a little but are still reasonable when one considers this is a 5-course meal. ****BEST BUY(13)

LE CYRANO, (French), 4134 Geary Blvd.(6th Av), 387-1090, 5-10:30pm, except Sun. Includes soup (onion or du jour), salad and dessert (cheese, mousse, maron-glace, ice cream or sorbet). Rack of lamb or NY pepper steak $15.50, frog legs in garlic butter $12.50, fish of day $11.50, deep fried rex sole $12, chicken in wine $10.50, calves sweetbreads in wine and cream sauce $12, beef in burgundy wine $11, cheese or mushroom omelette $8. Coffee, tea 75 cents. Reasonable prices for full dinner. ****BEST BUY(13)

ALEJANDRO'S (Mexican-Spanish), 1840 Clement (19th Av), 668-1184, 5-11pm. Paella for 2 $23.95-$24.95. Zarzuela (assorted seafood) $12.60, sopa de 7 mares with mushrooms (bouillabaisse Spanish-style) $12.60, rabbit cooked in natural juices and peanut sauce $11.95. Combination Mexican plates with rice, beans and salad $8.65-$9.45, flautos $8.15. Getting pricey but still highly recommended, especially for paella. ****BEST BUY(23)

KHAN TOKE THAI HOUSE, 5397 Geary Blvd. (23rd/24 Av), 668-6654, 5-11pm daily. The Thai royal-style dinner consists of fried fish cakes in cucumber sauce, spicy sour shrimp soup (served mild, medium or hot), sliced beef, choice of 2 entrees, dessert, Thai coffee or tea. Entrees are beef with red curry, peanuts, onions, coconut milk; marinated beef, peanuts, cucumber sauce; fried prawns in honey sauce; beef sauteed with mint leaves; filet of fish (hot). The a la carte menu includes exotic appetizers from $4.95-$5.95. The entrees, served with soup, range from $5.25-$9.95, e.g., prawns in honey sauce. Thai dancing every Sunday at 8:30. ****BEST BUY(13)

LUZERN (Swiss-French), 1431 Noriega, 664-2353. 5-10pm Wed-Sat, 4-9pm Sunday. Dinner includes soup, salad. dessert (creme caramel, ice cream or sherbet) and entree--poached salmon with shrimp sauce $11.25, veal with artichoke & mushrooms $11.75, duck with orange sauce $12.75, wienerschnitzel $11.75, rack of lamb $15.25. Intimate small, neighborhood restaurant. Considering the full menu, a reasonable price. ****BEST BUY(20)

PIERRE'S D'ANJOU (French), 2325 Taraval (33/34 Avs), 564-4464. 5-10pm except Mon. Lunch, includes soup or salad and coffee--e.g., filet sole or beef bourguignone $8.25, roast veal $9.55, petite steak $10.70. High for lunch but good. ****BEST BUY(20)

VERY GOOD***

DAVID'S DELI AND RESTAURANT (Jewish), 474 Geary (Taylor), 771-1600, 8am-1am daily. Dinner--$13.95 plus tax and service--consists of appetizer (chopped liver, gefillte fish, etc.) soup (barley, borsht, chav), entree (brisket, sauerbraten, stuffed cabbage, etc), cake from board (strudel, cheese, etc), coffee or tea. Pricey.***(1)

CAFE MAISONETTE (French), 315 8th Av (at Clement), 387-7992, 5:30-10pm Tues-Sat. Includes soup or salad, almond saffran rice and vegetables, e.g., breast of chicken tarragon $9.95, sweetbreads $13.95, escallop of veal $12.95. Salad: lettuce, cheese, walnuts $2.50. House wine, liter $6.95. ***(22)

TRICOLOR (French), 4233 Geary Blvd (6/7 Avs), 752-9974. 5-10pm Wed-Sat, 4-10pm Sun, closed Mon-Tues. Dinner includes soup, salad, ice cream, coffee. Roast pork, filet sole or coq au vin $11, frog legs $13, cordon bleu (veal with ham & cheese) $13.25, rabbit in white wine $15.25, broiled lobster $18. ***(13).

EL MANSOUR (Moroccan), 3123 Clement (31/32 Avs), 751-2312. One fixed meal only--soup, salad, bastelu, entree, dessert & mint tea $13.75. Entree is choice of couscous, chicken with prunes, or lamb with honey & almonds. Can make for an interesting evening. ***(23)

RIVE GAUCHE (French), 33 West Portal Ave, 566-0700. 5-10pm. Entrees served with soup or salad--sweetbreads $13.75, filets with pepper $14.75, duck with orange $13, rack of lamb $14.95. Chocolate mousse $3.50, crepes $4. ***(21)

VIII. Big Splurge Restaurants, $15-$30+

As stated in the Introduction, this section is designed either for the well-heeled or for the economically-minded who want to celebrate one Big Occasion, such as a birthday, wedding, the day they met, etc. Of course, when spending $15-$30+ per person, plus tax, tip and drinks (when not included in the price of the meal), one wants real value, right? Be assured I've chosen the Big Splurge restaurants with just that in mind. Please note that I've not given these restaurants star-ratings: they're all ****BEST BUY.

ZOLA'S (French), 1722 Sacramento (Polk/Van Ness), 775-3311. 6-10 Tues-Sat. Appetizers--salad of arugola, Belgian endive, pear & confit $4.50; mussels in saffron & curry cream $5, chevre with roasted garlic $5, dill-cured salmon $6. Entrees--cured pork loin with pernod cream, fennel & potatoes $14, cassoulet with sausage, duck & pork confit $14, rack of lamb with red wine & shallot sauce $16.50, duck breast in spices & chartreuse $16, loin of venison with cranberry confiture $17.50. Cheese $4, desserts $4.50, coffee or tea $1.25. Some wines in the $11-$17 range per bottle. This is elegant French dining in best tradition. This restaurant is still one of the all-time favorites of leading critics. (10)

THE HOUSE OF PRIME RIB, 1906 Van Ness Ave (Jackson), 885-4605. Prime rib dinner, $16.75, is served with salad, creamed spinach, mashed or baked potato, Yorkshire pudding and horseradish sauce. If the huge slab of luscious rib is not enough for you, ask for a bit more. This is about as good prime rib as you can get in the Bay Area and well worth the Big Splurge price. (10)

L'ESCARGOT (French), 1809 Union (Octavia), 567-0222. 5:30-10:30pm. Onion soup $3.25, crayfish-cream soup $3.50, pate $4, filet d'hareng $3.75. Dinners--served with soup *and* salad--sweetbreads with mushrooms & madeira $15.50, pork with apples and calvados sauce $15.75, roast rabbit with madeira & mustard sauce $15.75, duck with orange $16.50, poached salmon $16.50, rack of lamb $17.75. This elegant restaurant could qualify for the Splurge Section ($10-$15) since the dinners include soup *and* salad, but quality is definitely Big Splurge. A favorite. (5)

LE PIANO ZINC (French), 708 14th St (Market/Church), 431-5266. 6pm-midnight, Tues-Sun. The $25 Menu Gastronomique meal is the one to take. It changes from time to time. One example: lobster in cabbage leaves, grilled filet of swordfish in red wine & butter sauce, tournedos in bordelaise sauce, & a sumptuous dessert. You can also order a la carte with appetizers beginning at $4.25 (can be shared), entrees from $10 and desserts from $3.50. Good wines in the $12-$15 range. (15)

CAMARGUE (French), 2316 Polk (Union/ Green), 776-5577. 5:30-10pm, closed Mon. The $16 4-course prix-fixe dinner is a buy. A typical menu--which changes each month--ragout of snail with shitake mushrooms, green salad, cilantro crepe with smoked chicken, goat cheese & pine-nut sauce, or fish of day, & choice of dessert (e.g., white chocolate mousse with kiwi coulis). Food is artistically served. A la carte entrees are also reasonable, e.g., lamb $11, sauteed prawns $11. The biggest deal of all is the $35 wine-tasting 5-course dinner with 4 (yes, four!) wines, one for each course (except salad). This culinary delight is held every 2 months at the end of a month . Phone them and they will put you on the mailing list for the regular $16 & $35 menus. (10)

LE TROU (French), 1007 Guerrero (22nd St), 550-8169. 6:30-9pm Wed-Fri & Sun, 8pm (1-seating) Sat. On Thursday, Friday & Sunday there is a $30 5-course meal with 3 wines and on Saturday a $40 meal with 3 wines. Wednesday is a la carte. Since the owner, Robert Reynolds, also conducts a French cooking school on the premises, he likes to vary his menus, exploiting the different cuisines of France. Since you can get a week's menu in advance, you can choose according to your liking. Ring them up and they'll send a printed menu. A typical $30 meal--eggplant custard, duck in Marc, gnocchi with Muenster, kohlrabi with dill, Gewuerztraminer bavarian, coffee--and 3 wines. (16)

LE DOMINO (French), 2747 17th St (Bryant/Harrison), 626-3095. 5-10pm. Appetizers--duck pate with pistachios $4.50, herring in sour cream & wine sauce $3.95, bay shrimp salad $4.95, snails in chablis $5.25, onion soup $3.95. Dinner entrees include green salad, e.g., sweetbreads in vermouth $12.95, beef tongue ravigotte $10.95, medallions of veal in cream sauce $13.50, young rabbit in zinfadel $12.75, broiled lamb chops with herbs $14.95, sirloin steak with roquefort butter $14.95. French desserts $3.25-$4.25. A major feature of Domino's is the artistic presentation of the food. Sometimes, it looks too good to eat. (16)

GAYLORD (Indian), Ghirardelli Square, 771-8822. Here the big feasts are The Maharaja at $24.75 and The Maharani at $22.75, although you can also eat for less a la carte. The Maharaja includes soup (if you like it spicy, take Dal) tandoori chicken, 3 exotic lamb dishes (2 are tandoori) leavened bread, choice of Indian desserts, tea or coffee. If you don't want 3 lamb dishes, take the Maharani feast which omits the tandooris, has 1 lamb and 1 chicken dish, bread stuffed with onion, dessert, tea or coffee. You can eat a la carte by ordering soup ($2.75) or a fish hors d'oeuvres for 2 ($6) or a larger chicken, lamb or prawn dish ($12-$15). Tea or coffee are high at $2. My advice: if you want to Big Splurge, at least one of you take one of the feasts. Setting is luxurious, with a view of the Bay. (4)

MAMOUNIA (Moroccan), 4411 Balboa (45 Av), 752-6566. 6-10pm Tues-Sun. Dinner consists of one fixed meal for $14.50 or $16 consisting of a Moroccan appetizer, choice of entree, e.g., lamb with prunes or hare with paprika, mint tea and pastry. For $16 you get a salad & one more dish. This is the better deal if you're hungry enough. Setting is exotic. You sit on pillows on the floor and begin the meal by rinsing your hands in rose water.(20)

IX. Bars With Free Hors D'Oeuvres

We all know "there's no free lunch" but how about buying 1 (or 2) drink(s) for $1-$2.50 and eating all the hot and/or cold hors d'oeuvres you want at no extra cost? In checking this out I was amazed at the number of bars that offer free hors d'oeuvres, usually during the cocktail hours and Mon-Fri (but some on Saturday and a few even on Sunday). It's a pleasant way to pass the time, at little cost (If you don't drink too much, one drink is enough, especially if you're driving). The hors d'oeuvres range from potato chips or cheese and crackers only to hot & cold choices. Some resemble a small buffet supper. A word of caution: the price of drinks can be high, as much as $4.50 a drink at the posh hotels. I like the $1-$2.50 well-drinks range (somewhat higher for the plush-hotel bars), some double-size, so watch the price, especially in the large hotels or for fancy cocktails. Here are a number to choose from:

Note: Bars are listed roughly in order of distance from Union Square.

BY THE SQUARE (in Chancellor Hotel, Union Square), 362-2004. 5-7pm. Sandwiches & a hot dish. Well drinks $2.50. (1)

IRON HORSE, 19 Maiden Lane (Kearny/Grant), 362-8133. 5-8pm Mon-Sat. Hot & cold hors d'oeuvres. Well drinks $2.50. (1)

TEMPLEBAR, 1 Tillman Place (Post/Sutter off Grant Av), 362-6661. 5:30pm until food runs out, Mon-Fri. Free items vary, e.g., hot dogs, meatballs, chicken nuggets, salami, cheese & crackers, BBQ chicken legs. Well drinks $2.25. (1)

MAGIC PAN, 341 Sutter (Grant/Stockton), 788-7397. 5-7pm Mon-Fri. Nachos & tostados on Friday, otherwise varied. Well drinks & house wine $1.75, margaritas & Corona beer, Friday only, $2. (1)

RAGG'S, 22 4th St. (Mission/ Market), 777-0880. 5-7pm Mon-Fri. Chips & salsa, appetizers. Well drinks $2. (7)

WHITE ELEPHANT, 480 Sutter (Stockton, in Holiday Inn), 398-1331. 5-7pm. Hot hors d'oeuvres. Well drinks $2.50. (1)

FRONT PAGE, 20 Annie St. (3rd St/New Montgomery), 777-1955. 4-6pm. Hot & cold hors d'oeuvres. Well drinks $1.50. On Fridays a pianist plays light jazz. (7)

TONGA ROOM, Fairmont Hotel. 772- 5278. 5-7pm Mon-Fri. Chinese & Polynesian hors d'oeuvres, Friday all items. Well drinks $3.

CONFERENCE ROOM, 50 California (Market), 36th floor, 398-3722. 5-7pm Mon-Fri. Hot & cold hors d'oeuvres. Well drinks $2.75. (8)

VICTORIA STATION, 50 Broadway (Front), 433-4400. 5-7pm Mon-Fri--until food runs out. Potato skins, meat balls etc. Well drinks $2.50. (8)

MacARTHUR PARK, 607 Front St. (Jackson/Pacific), 398-5700. 5-7pm Mon-Fri. Meatballs, chicken, ribs, pate, dips & vegetables. Well drinks $2.50. (8)

CADILLAC BAR, 1 Holland (Mason/Howard), 543-8226. 4-7pm Mon-Fri. Mexican hors d'oeuvres. Well drinks $1.75. (7)

JAY'N BEE'S CLUB, 2736 20th St. (York), 648-0518. 5-6pm Mon-Thurs. Hot dogs, cold cuts, beans, salads. Well drinks $1.75. (17)

MAYE'S, 1233 Polk (Sutter), 474-7674. 3-6pm Mon-Fri. Cheeses, dips, hot dishes. Well drinks $1.25. (10)

CHEF YEE, 1695 Polk (Clay), 771-8989. 4-7pm (incl. Sat-Sun). Well drinks, wine & beer $1, hors d'oeuvres $1. (10)

LORD JIM'S, Polk & Broadway, 928-3015. 4-8pm Sun-Thurs. Hot & cold items. Well drinks $1.50. (10)

LA BARCA, 2036 Lombard (Fillmore/Webster), 921-2221. 4-6pm. Hot hors d'oeuvres. Well drinks (double) $2.50. (6)

X. Music, Film, Theater, Art

There is an abundance of free entertainment on the streets and in the parks of San Francisco. Each summer there are free concerts in Stern Grove and Golden Gate Park, classical, semi-classical, jazz. There are also jazz concerts at the Hyatt Regency Hotel. The area around 5th and Market, Fisherman's Wharf, and Ghiradelli Square abound in streetside entertainment (jazz, pantomime, etc.), for donations. This is also a great city for Little Theater and dance groups (both classical and modern). Consult the pink section of the *Sunday Examiner* for details, as well as the *Bay Guardian* and the free weekly programs of the Fort Mason Center and the public libraries.

Music

Classical

STERN GROVE CONCERTS, 558-4728, Stern Grove, 19th Ave. and Sloat Bvd. Co-sponsored but not funded by the San Francisco Recreation and Park Department. The 1987 season begins in June and continues through August. Watch the newspapers for details.

THE SAN FRANCISCO CONSERVATORY OF MUSIC, 1201 Ortega, 564-8086. Regular concerts, chamber and classical. They request a donation but will not turn away a poor student. Phone for details or watch the newspapers.

MORRISON ARTISTS' SERIES, San Francisco State University, School of Creative Arts, Chamber Music Center, 469-2176 or 469-1431. Professional chamber music. *Free.*

THE COMMUNITY MUSIC CENTER, 544 Capp St. (20-21st Sts), 647-6015. They have monthly programs; each concert is $2 for students and seniors, $4 for adults and $8 for small families. Phone for details.

OLD FIRST PRESBYTERIAN CHURCH, Sacramento and Van Ness, 474-1608. Concerts all year round. First-class performances of concert artists, trios and quartets, etc., classical chamber music. With an annual donation of $15 (tax deductible) you can attend all concerts at $1 each, $4 for others. Phone for details.

Jazz, Discotheques, Cafes

San Francisco is the home of wellknown jazz groups--e.g., Turk Murphy--and has dozens of jazz groups who perform nightly, as well as many discotheques. Some are expensive--e.g., Keystone Korner (but good!)--but many others are inexpensive, and some have no cover at all. To discover them yourself, stroll around North Beach, the Haight-Ashbury area, and Castro Street. Also, check the pink section of the *Sunday Examiner* and the *Bay Guardian* for listings. Here are some choices:

CAFE TRIESTE, 609 Vallejo (Grant), 392-6739. This is also a coffee house where opera singers serenade on Saturdays.

KIMBALL'S, 300 Grove, 861-5585. Jazz jam sessions.

TOSCA CAFE, 242 Columbus (Broadway), 986-9651. Opera records on juke box.

WOLFGANG'S 901 Columbus, 474-2995 or 441-4333. Jazz, rock, pop, folk music. funk.

CAFE FLORE, 2298 Market (Noe), 621-8579. Bar and restaurant. Gay-oriented.

MEATMARKET COFFEEHOUSE, 4123 24th (Castro), 285-5598. Gay area.

NETWORK COFFEEHOUSE,1329 7th Ave. (Irving), 664-2543. Discussions, lectures, music.

PAUL'S SALOON, 3251 Scott (Lombard/Chestnut),922-2456. Live bluegrass.

PLOWSHARES COFFEEHOUSE, Fort Mason, 441-8910. Live folk and other music, concerts.

LAST DAY SALOON, 406 Clement (5th Ave.), 387-6344. Rock, blues, country, western.

I-BEAM, 1748 Haight (Cole), 668-6006, 9 pm-2 am Mon-Sat and 6pm-2am Sun. New Wave disco with daily program that changes weekly.

NIGHTBREAK, 1821 Haight, 221-9008. Modern dance music, DJ and live, $3 entrance. Beer, wine and sake--no hard liquor--at reasonable prices. Sushi on Sundays.

HIGH CHAPARRAL, 2140 Market (Church), 861-7484. *No cover charge*. Country and Western music, as well as dance lessons. All the beer or soft drinks you can drink $4.

Opera, symphony, Ballet

San Francisco is world-famous in these fields, hence prices tend to be high for budget travelers (but not compared to Vienna and New York). The opera has stand-up tickets, while the symphony and ballet have afternoon performances with reduced prices for students. The symphony has open rehearsals. You can also buy half-price tickets often at S.T. B.S. at Union Square (see below). Phone for details, 864-3333 for Opera House and 431-5400 for Symphony.

Ballet

SAN FRANCISCO BALLET, 621-3838 (Box Office, Opera House). The San Francisco Ballet is internationally acclaimed. It uses the Opera House from about the middle of December to the beginning of May each year. Cheapest balcony seats are $5. Students and seniors with proper ID get half off on subscriptions for "orchestra sides", also on day of performance 2 hours before curtain time. There is standing room for all performances for $5. Also, you can sometimes get half off through S.T.B.S. (see below) on the day of performance.

S.T.B.S. Pronounced "stubs". This is a 1/2-price ticket office at the Stockton Street entrance to the Union Square garage. They offer day-of-performance tickets at 1/2 price, when available, as well as regular-price tickets for some shows. Phone 433-7827 for details.

Film

SAN FRANCISCO PUBLIC LIBRARY, 558-3191 (Information). Free monthly program available on request, for weekly films in 8mm, as well as lectures and talks, *free*.

GOETHE INSTITUTE, 530 Bush (Grant), 391-0370. This institute is subsidized by the German Government and has a library of German publications for public perusal. Also puts on free lectures and films, in the German language. Phone for free printed program.

BANK OF AMERICA, weekday noontime programs of films, travelogues, dance and music. They take place at the A.P. Giannini auditorium at the bank's world headquarters, 555 California Street. Call 953-1000 for a recording of the current week's program. *Free*.

Theater

Of the little theaters (99-seat capacity), highly recommended are the *One Act Theater* (421-6162), the *Magic Theater* (441-8822)--which is experimental and sometimes far-out--*Eureka* (558-9811) and *Theater Rhinoceros* (Gay, 861-5079). There are also ethnic theater groups, e.g., Chinese and Mexican. Most of these have previews at reduced prices, special offers, and sometimes free readings. Check the pink section of the *Sunday Examiner* for details.

 The A.C.T. (American Conservatory Theater), which is pricey and tends to favor conservative classics, has half-price tickets for students. Phone for details, 673-6440.

Art

San Francisco abounds in private galleries. Some have permanent collections of important Impressionists and Grand Masters. Most have periodic shows of new artists, either individual or collective shows. Consult the pink section of the *Sunday Examiner* for a complete listing of private galleries and their current shows. *Note*: a number of galleries, some of the largest and most impo rtant, are located on Sutter Street, between Powell and Van Ness. A stroll along Sutter Street can provide a rewarding afternoon. (For example, an interesting gallery for avant-garde modern ceramics is Dorothy Weiss Gallery, 256 Sutter Street).

XI. Museums

San Francisco has a plethora of Museums--art, science, ethnic (Chinese, Mexican, Italian, Jewish), Mint, wine, etc. Many are free while some are free on certain days of the week or month. Most are listed in the pink section of the Sunday Examiner, with details of current shows.

SAN FRANCISCO MUSEUM OF MODERN ART, Van Ness and McAllister, 863-8800. *Free* every Thurs from 6-10pm, otherwise adults $3, seniors and under 16 years of age $1.50, under 5 *free*. Open 10am-6pm Mon-Fri, 10am-5pm Sat-Sun.

M.H.DeYOUNG MUSEUM, 8th Ave. and Kennedy Drive, Golden Gate Park, 221-4811, Open 10am-5pm Wed-Sun. *Free* 1st Wed of the month and 10am. to noon on Sat. Otherwise $3 for adults, $1 for seniors (over 65) and ages 5 to 17. Admission is also good for the Asian Art Museum which is in the same building but has a different entrance. There is a permanent collection of the arts of Africa, Oceana and the Americas, as well as ancient and European art. *Free* docent tours.

ASIAN ART MUSEUM, same location as DeYoung, 668-8921, 1-5pm daily. Admission--which permits entrance to the DeYoung on days it is open--is the same as for DeYoung. *Free* 1st Wed of the month and 10am-noon on Sat.

PALACE OF THE LEGION OF HONOR, Lincoln Park, 221-4811. Open 10am-5pm Wed-Sun. *Free* First Wed of the month and 10 am to noon on Sat, otherwise same entrance charge as DeYoung. Permanent collection of French art; large Rodin sculpture collection. Out-of-town high-school students and undergraduate or graduate university students can obtain a oneyear admission pass for $5 to the Fine Arts Museums of San Francisco (DeYoung, Asian Art Museum, Palace of the Legion of Honor). This pass is available at the admission office of the Palace of the Legion of Honor. Students must present a valid student ID at the time of purchase.

CALIFORNIA ACADEMY OF SCIENCES, Golden Gate Park, 750-7145, from 10am5pm every day of the year. *Free* the first Wed of each month, otherwise adults $2, 611 75 cents, 1217 and seniors $1.

STEINHART AQUARIUM, California Academy of Sciences, Golden Gate Park, 7507145. The first Wednesday of the month is *free*. Open daily 10am-5pm. 14,500 live aquatic specimens. Dolphin feeding every 2 hours from 10:30am, penguin-feeding 11.30am and 4pm. Entrance fee included in Academy of Sciences ticket.

PLANETARIUM, in Academy of Sciences Building, but extra admission fee, 750-7141: adults $2; ages 5-17, seniors and students $1. Call 221-0168 for special shows.

EXPLORATORIUM, PALACE OF FINE ARTS, Lyon Street near Marina Blvd, 583-3200. A hands-on science, art and human perception museum. Open Wed from 1-9:30pm, Thurs and Fri from 1pm-5pm, weekends from 10am-5pm. Admission *free* first Wed of each month and every Wed after 6pm.

CABLE CAR MUSEUM, 1201 Mason (Washington), 474-1887, 10am-5pm daily. *Free.*

CALIFORNIA HISTORICAL SOCIETY, 2090 Jackson (at Laguna), 567-1848. Open Wed, Sat and Sun. from 1-4:30pm, guided tours at 1:30 and 3pm. First Sat of month *free.*

CALIFORNIA PIONEERS SOCIETY 456 McAllister Street, 861-5278. Gold Rush, early San Francisco silver, 19th century paintings. Wells Fargo stagecoach. Mon through Fri, 10am-4pm. *Free.*

CAROUSEL MUSEUM 633 Beach Street at Hyde, 928-0550. Finest examples of antique carousel art from 1880 to 1920. Daily 10am-6pm. $2.

CRAFTS AND FOLK ART MUSEUM, 626 Balbao, 668-0406. Open noon-5pm Wed-Fri, 1-4pm Sat and Sun.

CHINESE CULTURE CENTER, 750 Kearny (3rd floor of the Holiday Inn in Chinatown), 986-1822. They also sponsor the walking tours. Call for complete information. Open Tues-Sat, 10am-5pm. *Free.*

CHINESE HISTORICAL SOCIETY, 17 Adler Place (off Grant Ave), 391-ll88. Traces the history of the Chinese in America. Open Tues-Sat l-5pm. *Free.*

DIEGO RIVERA GALLERY, S.F. Art Institute. Open 9am-5pm daily. Features works of students and recent graduates. Has large enormous mural of Diego Rivera. *Free.*

ECONOMICS, at Federal Reserve Bank, 101 Market Street, 974-3252. A block-long exhibit of economic principles and history. Open Mon-Fri 9-4pm. *Free.*

FORT POINT NATIONAL, 556-1693. Open daily 10am-5pm. Fortress beneath Golden Gate Bridge. Rangers are on hand to explain the fort's history. *Free.*

ITALIAN AMERICAN MUSEUM, 673-2200. Fort Mason Center Building C. Contemporary Italian or Italian-American artists. Open noon-5pm Wed-Sun. *Free.*

JEWISH COMMUNITY MUSEUM, 121 Steuart St., 543-8880. Open 10 am-4pm Sun-Fri except Jewish holidays. *Free.*

LIBERTY SHIP. The Jeremiah O'Brien, last unaltered ship in operating condition. At Pier 3 East, Fort Mason Center, Bay and Laguna Streets. 441-3101. Open Mon-Fri 9am-3pm $2.

MARITIME MUSEUM, Beach St. at the foot of Polk, 929-0202. Open 10am-6 pm daily. Ranks as one of the great maritime museums of the U.S. *Free.*

OLD MINT, 5th and Mission, 974-0788. Open Mon-Fri, except holidays, 10am-4pm. Gold rush exhibits, gold, old coins, minting equipment, vaults. *Free.*

PHOTOGRAPHY MUSEUM, 47 Kearny St., Second floor, 392-1900. 15O years of photographic history. Open Mon-Fr, 9:30am-6pm. *Free.*

PRESIDIO ARMY MUSEUM, Lincoln and Funston Ave., in the Presidio, 561- 4115. Daily except Mon, 10am-4pm. Two hundred years of military and social history of the Presidio, including authentic uniforms and equipment. *Free.*

STRYBING ARBORETUM next to Hall of Flowers, 9th Ave. at Lincoln Way, 661-1316. Seventy landscaped acres, with over 6,000 different plant species in seasonal bloom. Weekdays 8am-4:30pm, weekends and holidays 10am-5pm. Tours daily at l:3Opm. *Free*.

TATTOO ART MUSEUM, 30 7th St. (near Greyhound Depot), 864-9798. Open 12-6pm daily. *Free*.

XII. Seeing the City Walking tours

San Francisco is best seen on foot. The city is divided into sections--geographical, historical, ethnic. There are many walking tours, some private, some city-run. The latter are free and are listed below. The private tours can be found in the pink section of the Sunday paper.

CITY GUIDE WALKS, 558-3981. These are led by volunteer city guides who are trained at the San Francisco History Room in the main library. No reservations are required. The tours start at 2pm and last about one hour. Each tour covers one specific area.

GOLDEN GATE PARK WALKS, 221-1311.Sponsored by the Friends of Recreation and Parks, these tours will begin on May 1st and run through October 31st, on Sat and Sun. Check by phone or look in the pink section of the Sunday paper.

COMMUNITY COLLEGE WALKS. Two hours beginning 10am on Sat. 239-3070.

XIII. Medical, Dental, Legal Aid

Travelers often need medical or dental care, sometimes on an emergency basis. Doctors and dentists are expensive. Emergency care at most hospitals and clinics is prohibitive. Taking care of a simple cut or wound in the emergency ward of a large hospital can cost over $100 (entrance fee, doctor's consultation, test for antibiotic reaction, dressing--all charged separately). Some travelers have insurance, some don't. There are alternatives, from moderate fees to free treatment. Also, San Francisco has a fair share of social medical services- for drug addiction, venereal disease, women's problems (including abortion), etc., at no-cost or low-cost. While there are drop-in hours at some clinics, it is always advisable to telephone and make an appointment.

AIDS PROBLEMS. Because of the importance of this subject, information has been included in this book. See *Hospice* in this section below. See also the *AIDS* listings under Miscellaneous below (*S.F. Aids Foundation, Shanti Project, Aids Interfaith Network*), as well as the *Gay Switchboard Operation Concern*.

AMERICAN CANCER SOCIETY, 545 Post (Mason), 673-7979, 9am-5pm. Free counseling, information, tests. Phone for appointment.

CLINICS. Most large hospitals have clinics which charge for services on a sliding scale. Usually, the scale is lower for San Francisco residents but they will probably accept a local address. Of course, you are then a "clinic patient" and there may be a long wait and brusquer treatment than if you were a private patient who paid a high fee. But you will get treated and you will pay much less than if you saw a doctor privately.

BUENA VISTA WOMEN'S SERVICES, INC., 2000 Van Ness (Broadway), 771-5000. First visit $35-$55. Abortion $210. Mon-Sat. Phone for appointment.

CALIFORNIA COLLEGE OFPODIATRIC MEDICINE, 1210 Scott, 563-3444. Free foot-screening examinations, 9 to 11am and 1:30 to 3:30pm Mon- Fri, 9-11am Sat. Initial office visit $22.

CENTRAL AID STATION, Health Department, City of San Francisco, 50 Ivy St. (Civic Center), 558-5432. 24-hour service, $12-$50 depending on service, which is much less than private physicians or most hospitals.

HAIGHT-ASHBURY FREE MEDICAL CLINIC, 558 Clayton (Haight), 431-1714. Phone for appointment. Includes VD testing. For drug-detoxification (529 Clayton), phone 621-2014, for Emergency (1696 Haight), 621-0140. Women's Need Section (1825 Haight), 221-7371. For information and referral or general help, phone Haight-Ashbury Switchboard (1338 Haight), 621-6211.

HEARING-DIAL-A-TEST, sponsored by the Hearing Society of the Bay Area. Dial 776-1291 to test your hearing.

HOSPICE, 401 Duboce (Church), 285-5619. This is an organization that deals with the terminally-ill, AIDS and non-AIDS. They provide 24-hour care on a teamwork basis--doctor, nurse, social worker, attendant, unpaid volunteer. The objective of Hospice is to permit a person to die in dignity, in his own home, and surrounded by his loved ones. *Hospice* also offers support to the family members, relatives, lovers, friends. I cannot speak too highly of this dedicated service. See also *S.F. Aids Foundation* and *Shanti Project* in *Miscellaneous* section below.

LYON MARTIN CLINIC, 2480 Mission (21 St), 641-0220. Health service for Bay area's lesbian community and women in general. Sliding scale, Medical & Medicare. Phone for information and appointment.

PACIFIC MEDICAL CENTER, Operation Concern, 1853 Market (Guerrero), 626-7000. Provides counseling for gays; gives legal, medical and therapeutic referrals.

PLANNED PARENTHOOD, 815 Eddy (Van Ness/Franklin), 441-5454. Examination and counseling, abortion (from $210), on a sliding scale. Phone for details.

PREGNANCY CONSULTATION CENTER, 1801 Bush (Octavia), 567-8757. Free pregnancy tests and counseling, 8;30am-4:30pm Tues-Sat. Phone for appointment.

SAN FRANCISCO GENERAL HOSPITAL, 1001 Potrero (22nd St), 821-8111. This is a city hospital. Admission rates to Emergency can run from $65 up, depending on the medical need, plus lab and x-ray fees. The same rates apply to the various clinics. However, no patient is turned away. If need is claimed, there is an eligibility interview *after* the treatment, on the basis of which the fee is determined. If a person is destitute, he or she will be charged nothing.

ST.ANTHONY'S CLINIC, 105 Golden Gatge Ave. (Jones), 864-0241. General medical 8:30am-10:30am Mon-Fri, by appointment Family clinic 1:30-4pm Mon, Wed and Fri. Phone for appointment. *Free*.

ST.LUKE'S NEIGHBORHOOD CLINIC, 1580 Valencia (Duncan), 641-6500. Mon-Fri, by appointment. Clinic is on sliding scale, according to need: $10-$18 plus x-ray and lab fees.

SUTTER MEDICAL GROUP, 1154 Sutter (Polk/Larkin), 441-6930, 8am to 8pm Mon-Fri, until 6pm Sat. Initial visit $42 (plus lab, x-ray, etc.) payable at time of visit. General medical only.

Dental

UNIVERSITY OF CALIFORNIA DENTAL CLINIC, 476-1891 or 476-5814 for Emergency. Fees are 1/3-1/2 of those charged by a private dentist. Hours: 8:15am sharp Mon-Fri, and 1:15pm sharp Mon-Thurs. Complete exam $10, x-rays of entire mouth $27, amalgan $15-$35.

UNIVERSITY OF THE PACIFIC SCHOOL OF DENTISTRY, 1255 Webster (Sacramento), 929-6500. Fees 1/3-1/2 that of private dentist. Emergency: Mon-Fri 9am or 2pm., otherwise 8:30am or 1:30pm Mon-Fri on a first-come-first-serve basis.

Legal

Foreign visitors are advised to apply to their consulates for free legal advice, where available (see Yellow Pages of telephone book under Consulates for phone number). If a consulate recommends a lawyer, bear in mind that the charge will be $50 and up per hour of consultation. An alternative would be to apply to a lawyer's guild or professional referral group, where a 1/2-hour consultation costs $20. This consultation can save much money in the long run.

NATIONAL LAWYER'S GUILD REFERENCE PANEL, 558 Capp (20-21 Sts), 647-5297. Charge for first half-hour $20.

S.F. BAR ASSOCIATION LAWYER REFERRAL SERVICE, 220 Bush (Sansome), 391-6102, $25 for first half-hour.

WOMEN AGAINST RAPE, 24-hour answering service, 647-7273.

LEGAL ASSISTANCE TO THE ELDERLY, 333 Valencia (14/15 Sts), 861-4444. Phone for information and referral.

HYATT LEGAL SERVICES, 17 Drumm (Market), 781-4666. This is a nationwide organization that employs young lawyers. They charge $20 for a first consultation and have fixed fees for such things as wills and other services.

XIV. Miscellaneous A-Z

AIDS and ARC (AIDS Related Condition)

San Francisco has been hit hard by the AIDS epidemic. Heroic measures are being taken to keep the disease from spreading and to help those affected, Gays and heterosexuals. Some 18 different organizations have become active in this. Here are some of the more important ones:

SAN FRANCISCO AIDS FOUNDATION, 821-1230. Initiates and coorinates AIDS prevention projects in the Bay Area for the general public and for people at high risk for AIDS. Also provides and coordinates direct social services, referrals, emergency housing, foodbank services for people with AIDS and ARC in San Francisco (863-4376). Operates a 24-hour *Hot Line* (863-AIDS) where open and confidential information can be had at all times.

SHANTI PROJECT, 558-9644. Provides emotional support programs for persons with AIDS, their friends, lovers, and families, as well as non-counselling practical support such as transportation, shopping and housekeeping to persons with AIDS. Also, provides long-term low-cost group housing for persons with AIDS. *Note*: When the AIDS patient becomes bed-ridden, *Shanti* usually turns him/her over to Hospice for round-the-clock medical care. See *HOSPICE* in Medical section above.

AIDS INTERFAITH NETWORK, 928-HOPE. Provides spiritual support and counselling to persons with AIDS, their families, lovers and friends. Also, provides education and training to the religious community at large regarding AIDS.

CHURCH GROUPS. Practically all Church groups in San Francisco have special programs for AIDS-afflicted persons in their communities and provide, particularly, bereavement counselling and services. For information apply to the Church of interest. Special mention is made of the following:

AIDS AND ARC PROGRAMS OF CATHOLIC SOCIAL SERVICE, 50 Oak St. (Market), 864-7400 ext. 26. Headed by Father Michael Lopes. Emergency help and referral for persons with AIDS or ARC, their families and loved ones.

THE HOPE/HELP CENTER OF THE PARSONAGE, Episcopal Diocese of California, 555-A Castro (18/19 Sts), 861-HOPE or 800-AID-TALK. This is a church or spiritual resource center for persons with AIDS or ARC, their families, lovers, friends. It is part of a national spiritual network. They work closely with other AIDS groups for exchange and referral.

HOSPICE. See under Medical section above.

OPERATION CONCERN. See below under Gay Switchboard.

Books, New

Here are some stores offering discounts or bargains:

A WRITER'S BOOK STORE, 2848 Webster (Union) 921-2620.

BONANZA INN, 650 Market (Sutter/Post), 392-7378. Many specials, particularly art books. Also see under Foreign Newspapers.

BOOKS, INC, 140 Powell (Ellis) 397-1555 and 3515 California (Locust), 221-3666.

CITY LIGHTS, 261 Columbus Ave. (Broadway), 362-8193. A literary meeting place.

COLUMBUS BOOKS, 540 Broadway (Columbus), 986-3872; 84 4th St. (Moscone Center), 896-0611.

CROWN BOOKS, 5198 Castro (18 St), 552-5213, 740 Clement (8/9 Avs), 221-5840, 1245 Sutter (Polk/Van Ness), 441-7479. All books discounted.

DALTON B., 200 Kearny (Sutter), 397-5955 and 2 Embarcadero Center, 982-4278. Especially art books and best-sellers.

DOUBLEDAY, 140 California (Front), 421-7822 and 265 Sutter (Grant/Kearny), 989-3420.

EUROPEAN BOOK STORE, 500 Sutter, (Powell), 362-4812 and 925 Larkin (Geary/Post), 474-0626.

FOLEY BOOK STORE, 119 Sacramento (Drumm), 982-7766. All books discounted.

HUNTER'S BARGAIN BOOKSTORE, 151 Powell St, (O'Farrell), 397-5955 Very larges election at bargain prices.

THE KINOKUNIYA BOOKSTORE OF AMERICA, 1581 Webster (Japantown), 567-7625. Complete collection of Japanese, Asian and American books.

PAPERBACK TRAFFIC, 1501 Polk (California), 771-8848. Large selection of gay themes.

RAND McNALLY, 595 Market (2nd St), 777-3131. Travel books & maps.

STACEY'S, 581 Market (2nd St), 421-4687. Large economic section.

WALDENBOOKS, see phone book for stores.

Books, Second-Hand

There are a number of second-hand book shops in San Francisco. Check the Yellow Pages of the phone book for locations near you. Most of these shops also sell new books, often at discount. Here are a few good ones:

McDONALDS'BOOKSHOP, 48 Turk (Market), 673-2235.

ALBATROSS BOOK STORE, 166 Eddy (Taylor), 885-6501.

GREEN APPLE BOOKS, 506 Clement (6th Ave.), 387-2272.

ROOKS AND BECORDS, 2222 Polk (Vallejo), 771-7909. Also used records.

ART GALLERY, 518 Haight (Fillmore), 861-2989. Including used art and music books.

PHOENIX, 3870 24 St. (Church), 821-3477. Books and records.

Cafe, European

CAFE' WITTGENSTEIN, 2150 Chestnut St. (Pierce/Steiner), 921-8834. Walter Menrath, a practising psychologist and educator, has realized the dream of a lifetime by opening a genuine Viennese coffeehouse, with all the trimmings--including wine, beer, aperitifs--like the kind he knew well when he lived in Vienna. He will also use the facility for literary and artistic events such as readings, concerts, art exhibits. Definitely worth a visit if you'd like your espresso and pastry with *Schlagoberst* (whipped cream), in true Viennese or English tea style. Also good for breakfast, lunch and an extended afternoon coffee sitting.

Cafes, Literary

Here are 4 cafes where you can read a book or newspaper--available free--sip a cup of coffee and mingle with interesting young people. Prices are not uniformly cheap but small items are available.

CHATANUGA CAFE, 1608 Haight (Clayton), 552-5526. A young-persons' hangout. Tea, coffee, sandwiches, lunches and dinners. Prices are reasonable.

CLARION , 2118 Mission (17th/18th Sts), 552-4393. Cafeteria-style.

CAFE PICARO, 3210 16th (Valencia/Guerrero), 431-4089.

CAFE EUROPA, 362 Columbus (Vallejo), 986-8177. Excellent salads as well as usual cafe fare.

THE BOOKPLATE, 2080 Chestnut (Steiner), 563-0888, soups, salads, sandwiches, quiche.

CAFE BABAR, 994 Guerrero (22 St), 282-6789. A casual meeting place for a glass of wine. Frequented by local poets, musicians, writers, filmmakers etc.

Clothing, New and Used

There are a number of factory outlets and wholesale-retail bargain clothes shops for men and women. For listings, see the telephone Yellow Pages under *Clothing* or *Clothing Used,* or consult the latest edition of *Bargain Hunting in the Bay Area* by Sally Socolich, which is in most book stores.

Credit Cards

Most Europeans who carry credit cards come to the U.S. with *American Express*. This is a mistake as far as San Francisco is concerned because many shops, restaurants and department stores will not take *American Express* but will take *Visa* or *Mastercard* (in Europe, *Eurocard*). Many gas stations will not accept credit cards, only cash. Those who do, charge more than for cash.

Daily Events in Five Languages

THE SAN FRANCISCO CONVENTION AND VISITORS BUREAU gives you tips on daily events and sightseeing in French (391-2003), German (391-2004), Spanish (391-2122), and English (391-20010), Japanese (391-2101).

Dial

*Note:*See phone-book for complete listings.

DIAL-a-PRAYER, 664-7729. Prayers and readings from the Bible.

DIAL-the-CORRECT TIME, 767-8900.

DIAL-the-WEATHER REPORT, 936-3212.

Evensong

GRACE CATHEDRAL EPISCOPAL CHURCH, 1051 Taylor (California), at the top of Nob Hill, 776-6611, a place where the services are sung, every Thursday at 5:15pm, at other hours on holidays, by the Grace Men's Choir and the Boy's Choir (during the school year). A lovely, peaceful and inspiring experience for those so inclined.

Film Developing and Printing

The prices vary considerably, 15-50 cents a print. *Walgreen's* and *Merrill's* drugstore chains do a passable job at discount prices, as do the *Safeway* and *Lucky's* supermarkets. There are several chains who offer special prices from time to time ,e.g., *Fotomat Co, Fox Photo,* and *Sun Photo* whose various locations are listed in the phone book.

SAN FRANCISCO PHARMACY, 160 Sutter (Kearny/ Montgomery), 956-3784. Has a large film-developing and printing operation at discount prices.

Food for the Indigent

Lost your wallet or your job and don't have enough for a meal? There are several dining rooms open to the destitute, no questions asked. Also check Traveler's Aid Society of S.F., 38 Mason (Market), 781-6738, for more listings, as well as low-cost housing and eating.

St.ANTHONY'S DINING ROOM, 45 Jones (Market), 552-3838, 10am-12:30pm.

ST.FRANCIS MEAL SERVICE, 432 Mason (Post), 392-7463. 11am-12:15pm. Also at YWCA, 620 Sutter, 2nd floor, 11am-12:15pm 7 days a week.

GLIDE CHURCH, 330 Ellis (Taylor), 771-6300, 8-9am, 12-1pm, 4-5:30pm Mon-Fri, weekends breakfast & lunch only.

Foreign Newspapers and Magazines

HAROLD'S, 599 Post (Taylor), 474-2937.

CASTRO KIOSK, 548 Castro (18/19 Sts), 431-3323.

EUROPEAN BOOK COMPANY, 500 Sutter (Powell), 362-4812 and 925 Larkin (Geary and Post), 474-0626.

BONANZA INN, 650 Market, (Sutter/Post), 392-7378

Gasoline

If you are driving, it pays to check the stations. The cheapest are usually the self-service variety. Stations vary as much as 20 cents a gallon. At the moment, the cheapest is ARCO which has many stations around town. Compare!

Gay Switchboard

OPERATION CONCERN, 1853 Market (Guerrero) outpatient office of Pacific Medical Center, 626-7000. Provides counseling for gays; gives legal, medical and therapeutic referrals. Special program for seniors. See also listings under *AIDS* above, also under *Hospice* in Medical section.

Golden Gate Park

Numerous activities take place in the Golden Gate Park--concerts, athletic events, walks, exhibits, shows, plays etc. For a detailed listing of such events, see the Sunday edition of the *San Francisco Progress,* the pink section of the *Sunday Examiner* and the *Bay Guardian.*

Gospel Service

For an unusual and moving experience, attend a Sunday morning service at the GLIDE CHURCH, corner Ellis and Taylor (opposite Airporter Terminal).

Haight-Ashbury Switchboard

SWITCHBOARD, 1338 Haight (Masonic/Central), 621-6211. This switchboard handles all problems of survival: medical, legal, drugs & cheap transportation (share-rides), etc.

Hairdressers, Barbers

Most everyone needs a haircut now and then. Prices are high in San Francisco, as elswhere, but if you wash your own hair (the same day), you can get a good, styled haircut for $6--$8 at the following:

GREAT HAIRCUTS, $6. See phone book for listings.

THE HAIRCUT PLACE, 1622 Polk (Clay), 673-8313. $6.

There are a number of barber colleges and beauty-culture schools in downtown San Francisco. Sometimes they are not bad, while some are almost professional Some are free but others can turn out to be expensive, so be sure to clarify the price before starting. In all cases, phone for an appointment. Check the Yellow Pages of the phonebook under *Beauty Culture Schools* for locations and phone numbers.

Ice Cream

Everybody's favorite. For my money, the best ice cream is the ultra-chocolate at *Double Rainbow*. For location nearest you see the phonebook. Price is high: one large scoop $1.25. Other good ice creams are *Mitchell's* (local, very good), *St. Francis* (local, extra good), *Swensens, Bud's, Dreyers, Haagen-Dazs,* and various Italian gelatos. You'll find them listed in the Yellow and White Pages of the phone book.

Japanese Activities

For general information on the shops, restaurants, and theater in the Japan Center, phone 567-6076.

Laundry and Dry Cleaning

Most neighborhoods have laundromats where you can wash and dry while you wait. Just ask around or check the Yellow Pages of the phonebook. The same holds for dry cleaning, although some are much more expensive than others. I can recommend two whose prices and quality are good:

VEL CLEANERS, 485 O'Farrell (Jones), 474-4135.

COME CLEAN CENTER, 3320 Fillmore (Lombard), 922-2040. 8am-8pm. Coin-operated, with attendant assistance. $8 for 8 lbs. Convenient--and cheap--when you have a mixed bag of sweaters, ties, slacks, etc.

Money Exchange

If possible, exchange at banks, not hotels.

Municipal Railway (MUNI) Bus Map

You can usually get a free bus map at the MUNI head office at Presidio Ave. and Geary Blvd (Opposite Sears), but phone first to see if they are available, 673-6864. A *MUNI Street and Transit Map* can be purchased at most bookstores and newspaper stands for $1.25.

Natural Foods and Vitamins

There are a number of shops in San Francisco; they are listed in the Yellow Pages of the phone book under Health Foods and Vitamins. There are several vitamin shops on lower Market St. and several on Polk St., also a number in the Mission and Haight St. areas. Here are a few:

BUFFALO WHOLE FOOD & GRAIN CO., 1058 Hyde (California), 474-3053.

GENERAL NUTRITION CENTER, see phone book for listings. Mostly vitamins, packaged food.

GREAT EARTH VITAMINS, see phone book for listings.

RAINBOW GROCERY, corner of 15th and Mission, 863-0620. I consider this the best in town, stocks all kinds of fruit, vegetables and health food, vitamins in bulk, etc.

REAL FOOD COMPANY, see phone book for listings. Especially good for fruit & vegetables.

SEEDS OF LIFE, 1465 Haight (Masonic), 626-7288. Very large selection, good prices.

Phonograph Records, New and Used

AQUARIUS RECORDS, 3961 24th St. (Sanchez), 647-2272. New and used.

DISCOUNT RECORDS, 656 Market (2nd St) ,398-4574. New.

McDONALD'S BOOKSHOP, 48 Turk (Market), 673-2235.

RECORD FACTORY, see phone book for listings.

THE RECORD VAULT, 2423 Polk (Union/Filbert), 441-1386. New and used.

ROOKS & BECORDS, 2222 Polk (Vallejo), 771-7909. Used.

TOWER RECORDS, Columbus & Bay (Fisherman's Wharf area), 885-0500. New.

Photocopies

For single copies. there are machines in Woolworth's, post offices and drugstores at 10-15 cents per copy. For multiple copies, there are 5-cent copying centers in various parts of the City. They also provide a variety of printing services. Consult the Yellow Pages for shops nearest you. Here are a few:

COPY CIRCLE, 1701 Polk (Clay), 474-5757.

PIP PRINTING, See phonebook for locations. There are a number around town and they provide good, low-price services, including 5-cent photocopies.

CARBON ALTERNATIVE. See phonebook for locations.

Post Office

All branch post offices are open from 9am-5:30pm weekdays, and some are open on Saturday 9am-1pm. Rincon Annex, 99 Mission at Spear, is open on weekdays from 8am to 10pm and on Saturday 9am-5pm. Conveniently, the post office in MACY'S on Union Square is open on Sundays from 11am-5pm.

Radio

CLASSICAL MUSIC STATIONS. The following two stations play classical music all day, interspersed with low-key advertising: KDFC, 102.1 FM and KKHI, 95.7 FM.

KQED, FM 88.5, a public radio station of high quality. No advertising. News reported 5-9am and 4-7pm.

NATIONAL PUBLIC RADIO. Station KALW, 91.7 FM. This station is free of advertising and presents high-caliber news reporting (7-9am and 5-6pm), symphonies, opera etc. This station is of particular interest to foreign travelers as it reports extensively on foreign events in the morning, switching to BBC at 9am. A free quarterly program can be obtained by phoning 648-1177.

COUNTRY MUSIC RADIO, KSAN, 94.7 FM.

JAZZ RADIO, KFAZ, 92.7 FM; KPFA, 94.1 FM.

ROCK RADIO, KMEL,106 FM; KOME, 98.5 FM; KTIM, 100.9 FM; KQAK, 98.9 FM; KFOG, 194.5 FM.

Recreational Vehicle Park

SAN FRANCISCO R.V. PARK, 196 sites, 250 King St. (3rd/4th Sts), 986-8730, $24 per night for 2, plus $2 each additional person from age 5.

Senior Citizens

ADULT INFORMATION SERVICE, 558-5512. For all kinds of information, for lists of discounts on goods and services, for reduced fares (a driver's licence with photo on it, showing age 65 and over, is required). Information can also be obtained from the following: Catholic Office on Aging, 864-4044; Lutheran Care for Aging, 441-7777; Jewish Center, 346-6040.

Shoe Repair

Actually, you can buy a pair of shoes for what some ask to repair full soles and heels--up to $35. Here are some shoe repair shops where the prices are less than the general run:

VETERAN SHOE SERVICE, 2138 Irving (22nd Ave), 664-3046. Men's heels $7, half soles and heels $21, full soles and heels from $25. Women's heels from $3.50, soles from $10.

STAN'S SHOE REPAIR, 1056 Fillmore, (Golden Gate). Heels--women's $4.50, men's $6.95; 1/2 soles--women's $12.50, men's $17.50; full soles and heels--women's $16.50, men's $24.95. 10% discount for seniors and students. Very good workmanship.

Student Information, Services

INTERNATIONAL VISITOR'S CENTER, 312 Sutter (Grant),986-5454.

Traveler's Aid

TRAVELER'S AID, 38 Mason (near Market), 781-6738. Established to help travelers in need.

Telephone for Long Distance or Overseas

If you have access to a private phone, you can direct-dial to most parts of the world or ask the operator for person-to-person calls. Phoning from a hotel is much more expensive. Calls to most overseas locations are cheaper from 6pm to 7am. Check the telephone book for details and rates or call the operator. The same holds true for long-distance calls within the United States. Lower evening rates are from 5pm-11pm and lowest night rates are from 11pm-8am, Mon-Fri and all day Sat-Sun.

XVI. Ethnic Restaurants

* Especially recommended

ARGENTINE
La Olla, 41, 90

ARMENIAN
Little Omar, 54

BASQUE
Des Alpes, 96
The Basque Hotel, 96
Cafe du Nord, 96
*Obrero, 96

BRAZILIAN
De Paula's, 68

BURMESE
*Mandalay, 82

CARIBBEAN
Welcome Mat, 89
*Prince Neville's, 81

CHINESE
See also Low-Priced Chinese
Lunches, 40

A-1, 60
Asia Garden, 69
Cafe Orient, 35
Canton, 36
Canton Tea House, 69
Chung King, 77
Food Center, 42
Fook, 69, 91
*Franthai, 56
Golden Dragon, 56
Golden Key, 86, 101

Golden Palace, 36
Grand Palace, 69
Great Wall, 56
Hang Ah, 69
Harbin, 89
Hong Kong, 57
Hon's Won-Ton, 56
Hunan Court, 87
Hunan Village, 78
Jade Garden, 100
Jing Kiung, 53
Jung's, 36
*King of China, 69
King Tin, 77
Kum Ling, 61
Kum Moon, 61
Kum Shan, 70
Lotus Garden, 106
Lung Fung, 85
*Narai, 84
New Golden Palace, 36
Ocean, 91
Ocean Garden, 60
Ocean Sky, 57, 77
Pot Sticker, 77
Red Crane, 101
Riverside, 102
Royal Kitchen, 59, 67
*Sam Woh, 56
San Wong, 81
Silver, 59
*Silver Moon, 101
*Sun Hung Yuen, 77
Sun Ya, 60
Szechuan Village, 89
*Tai Chi, 78
Ton Kiang, 83, 101
*Tsing Tao, 85
*Tung Fong, 69
Uncle, 53
*Vegi Food, 107
Wah Do, 57
Yank Sing, 70
Yet Wah, 91
*Yuet Lee, 78
Yu Nan, 91

XVI. Glossary of Asian & Mexican Cuisines

San Francisco has over 4,000 restaurants. The Chinese restaurants are by far the largest group, followed by Italian, Central-American, Vietnamese, Thai & Japanese. Most of us like to explore new cuisines but often lack the elementary knowledge which is required if our visit to a new (to us) ethnic restaurant is to be a success. Even experienced travelers who are used to new culinary adventures often have embarrasing experiences. Not long ago sophisticated European friends visited a Chinese restaurant for the first time in their lives. They wanted to try various dishes, beginning with an exotic-sounding soup. Since they were 3, they ordered 3 soups and were promptly served with 3 huge bowls, each enough for 4 persons! The waiter was a bit surprised at the order but assumed these were diners of very hearty appetites. He could not know they had ordered a la European, namely, one order of soup per person....Another problem is that many ethnic menus assume the diner knows the nomenclature. Often the curious diner is not even aware of the *kind* of food he would be getting. Perhaps this modest beginning of a Glossary for Asian and Central-American cuisines will be of help.

Chinese

The Chinese cusine ranks among the best in the world. Some place it even above the French & Italian. Since China is such a large country, there are regional differences in climate and foods, hence different cuisines have developed. One can divide the cuisines into four major types: *Cantonese, Mandarin, Szechuan* and *Mongolian. Cantonese* is endemic to southern China. Here the food is lightly-seasoned, and quickly stir-fried. Thus, the crispness in the vegetables is preserved and the meats remain tender and tasty. *Mandarin* dishes are spicier, more seasonings are used, including an abundance of garlic and onions. *Szechuan* food is noted for its full-flavor and many dishes are considered "hot", i.e., prepared with chiles. *Mongolian* cuisine uses lamb a good deal, which is often prepared over indoor barbecue devices. There are other sub-categories, e.g., *Hakka* cuisine which derives from a mountain tribe near Canton. This cuisine uses wine in the preparation of some dishes. Another cuisine is *Hunan* which is similar to *Szechuan*, i.e., "hot".

As we all know, the Chinese use chopsticks instead of cutlery in eating their food. As a result, all Chinese food is prepared in "small bites", so that it can be handled by chopsticks. Another characteristic of Chinese food is that it is prepared in such manner that a small group can have at least a number of dishes, often at least 5-6. A Chinese meal contains no bread, butter or salad. It usually begins with an appetizer--egg rolls, BBQ ribs etc.--then the main dishes, and rice or noodles. The only recommended cold beverage to drink is beer (although American often drink wine with the meal, which I do not recommend). The Chinese drink tea at the end of the meal but in the U.S., the Chinese restaurants serve tea throughout the meal, which I personally find good.

Some popular Chinese dishes (beginning with appetizers) are--*chungun,* spring or egg rolls made of pancakes with pork-shrimp or chicken filling; *won ton,* Chinese ravioli with various fillings; *chow mein,* noodles either fried crisply or boiled, with various meats or fish; *egg drop soup;* egg-flower soup; braised fish; shrimp in black bean sauce; chicken and almonds or walnuts; fried or roast duck; sweet and sour pork, beef, shrimp or fish; stir-fried vegetables; rice or noodles with pork, shrimp, fish etc. Most food in Chinese restaurants is prepared *after* it is ordered, in woks (cone-shaped pans which store enormous heat and permit very fast cooking, which is the secret of Chinese cooking).

Mexican, Central-American

San Francisco has many Central-American restaurants, mostly Mexican. The other cuisines--e.g., Salvadoran, Nicaraguan, Cuban--are similar to Mexican and use similar ingredients. Here is a listing of the more popular dishes: *Tacos*--crisp corn tortillas folded & filled with beef, chicken or pork, lettuce, tomatoes & grated cheese. *Tostados*--open-face, crisp corn tortillas covered with chicken, beef or pork, lettuce, tomatoes & grated cheese. *Burritos*--flour tortilla rolled &

filled with beef, pork or chicken. *Enchiladas*--soft corn tortillas dipped in a mild red sauce and stuffed with cheese, chicken, beef or pork and topped with sour cream, lettuce & grated cheese. *Chile relleno*--giant Mexican green pepper (not hot), stuffed with Monterey Jack cheese and topped with salsa. *Carnitas*--seasoned chunks of pork deep-fried and topped with tomatoes and onions. *Flautas*--rolled crisp tortillas stuffed with beef or chicken and topped with sour cream and guacamole (avocado dip). *Steak ranchero*--sauteed beef with bell peppers, onions, tomatoes and mild salsa. *Machaca*--chunks of beef, scrambled with eggs. *Spanish omelette*--made with mild salsa, bell pepper, onions and tomatoes. *Birria*--stew. *Menudo*--tripe.

Thai(Siamese)

Thai dishes are among the spiciest in the world. The dominant spices used are coriander, lemon grass, citrus juice, tamarind, garlic, basil and chiles. Staples are fresh vegetables, fish and rice. They also use peanuts, coconut milk and curries, as does the cuisine of India. The green curries are the hottest. But they also have mild dishes, particularly the noodle salads with carmelized sauce and shrimp. Also, the egg rolls filled with rice and shrimp or crab. They also have mild soups, light salads and steamed dishes for the more timid. The Thais do not use chop sticks but eat with fork and spoon (no knife). They drink tea or beer during or after the meal. Desserts are novel, e.g., the liquid desserts of pureed fruits or the puddings made with sago (tapioca) or rice flour.

Japanese

A typical Japanese meal begins with *sake* (rice wine) served warm. Japanese observe a great deal of ceremony in serving and drinking the sake, as they do in setting the table and in serving and drinking tea. Food is regarded as an esthetic experience, hence a typical Japanese meal will contain much artistic detail. For example, a tiny but perfect sliver of carrot is placed in clear consomme and meat is arranged with mathematical precision. Soups are clear (suimono) or in a base of fermented beans and malt (*miso-shiru*). *Tempura* is deep-fried food. *Sukiyaki* is chicken or beef with soy sauce, pan-fried with vegetables and Japanese noodles. The Japanese like to finish a meal with a bite of pickle (*konomon* or *daikon*) made from the giant white radish which is about 3-feet long. Some everyday Japanese dishes are *udon* (a wheat-flour noodle), *tofu* (a soybean curd), *soba* (buckwheat noodles), *gohan* (boiled rice), *nimame* (boiled beans)., *yosenabe* (a soup containing fish, meat, vegetables). Japanese green tea is the favorite beverage.

Vietnamese

This cuisine is similar to Thai but milder.(Chiles are used a lot, however, in southern Vietnam). There is a similarity to Chinese cooking as well, especially in the spring rolls (*cha gio*) which are made from bean sprouts, bean threads, pork & crabmeat wrapped in transparent rice paper and fried. The cuisine uses coriander, lemon grass, mint and basil, like the Thai. The most important ingredient is a pungent flavoring made from fermented anchovies, other small fish and salt, called *nuoc mam*. The Vietnamese use this in almost every dish, together with garlic, shallots, sugar and chiles as a dipping sauce which is called *nuoc sham*. The Vietnamese use chopsticks and eat family-style, like the Chinese. A typical meal would consist of one or two appetizers, soup, and 4-5 main dishes, for 4 or more persons. Some favorite Vietnamese dishes are--*chao tom*, ground seasoned shrimp served on skewers. *Sup man cua*, a creamy asparagus and crabmeat soup flavored with *nuoc mam* and pepper; *Ga xao sa ot* is chicken sauteed with lemon grass, chile and fish sauce; also known as "singing chicken"; *ca chien*, deep-fried fish; *ca hap*, steamed fish garnished with pork, ginger, scallions, pickled cabbage and tomatoes; *nem nuong*, barbecued pork balls, served with peanut sauce; *tom rim*, shrimp in a sauce of carmelized sugar and seasoned with pepper. There is also a fondue dish, *thit bo nbung dam*, which consists of raw slices of beef dipped in a flavored beef stock and often eaten with scallions and vegetables wrapped in rice paper. Due to the French influence, the Vietnamese often drink wine with their meals but tea, beer and coffee are also popular.

XVII. Index